THERESA
MAY

Virginia Blackburn is an author and journalist, who has written more than forty books including novels, biographies, art critique and an investment guide. She is currently a columnist on the *Daily Express* and has written across the national press including *The Times*, the *Sunday Times*, the *Daily Telegraph*, *The Spectator* and the *Financial Times*. She was brought up in the United States, Germany and the UK and read English Literature at the University of Cambridge. She lives in London.

THERESA MAY

The Downing Street Revolution

VIRGINIA BLACKBURN

JOHN BLAKE

Published by
John Blake Publishing Limited,
3 Bramber Court, 2 Bramber Road,
London W14 9PB, England

www.johnblakebooks.com

www.facebook.com/johnblakebooks
twitter.com/jblakebooks

First published in paperback in 2016

ISBN: 978-1-78606-264-2

British Library Cataloguing-in-Publication Data:
A catalogue record for this book is available from the British Library.

Design by www.envydesign.co.uk

Printed in Great Britain by CPI Group (UK) Ltd

1 3 5 7 9 10 8 6 4 2

Text copyright © Virginia Blackburn 2016

Papers used by John Blake Publishing are natural, recyclable products made from
wood grown in sustainable forests. The manufacturing processes conform to the
environmental regulations of the country of origin.

Every attempt has been made to contact the relevant copyright-holders, but some
were unobtainable. We would be grateful if the appropriate people could contact us.

This book is dedicated to the
memory of John Antcliffe

CONTENTS

1

BREXIT

Friday morning, 24 June 2016, and all across the United Kingdom of Great Britain and Northern Ireland, the nation was waking up in shock. The day before, the public had voted in a referendum with a very simply worded question, 'Should the United Kingdom remain a member of the European Union or leave the European Union?', with two responses: 'Remain a member of the European Union' or 'Leave the European Union'. Despite heavy campaigning from the Leave side, the received wisdom had been that Britain would vote to Remain. The uncertainty involved in leaving was deemed to be just too great and so the nation went to bed, duly setting their alarms for the following morning in the near-certain expectation of hearing that, by a slim majority, the UK had opted to remain part of the EU.

But in possibly the biggest political upheaval in at least half a century, the public had not done as it was told. Despite the entire weight of the establishment, on both right and left, promoting the cause to remain, so-called 'Project Fear' being ramped up to ever greater levels with threats of emergency budgets, increased taxes and slashed public spending, interventions by even the US President, Barack Obama, that the UK would be sent 'to the back of the queue' should it venture to say goodbye to the EU, over 17 million people, a majority of 51.89 per cent of the unprecedentedly high turnout, had decided to go. The sense of shock was palpable. Hardly had the ballot boxes closed and the results been announced than there was a distinct feeling in the air that said, 'What have we done?' Stunned newscasters sounded as if they could hardly believe the news they were reading. Across the globe other countries and political leaders expressed absolute incredulity that Britain could have taken such a momentous step.

It was the start of a month in politics that was like nothing the country had experienced in decades. Some early commentators compared it to the Suez Crisis but it quickly became obvious that it was far more serious than that. That first Friday morning set the tone for what was to follow: as one seismic shock followed on from the next, the Prime Minister, David Cameron, emerged from the door of Number 10 Downing Street and addressed the cameras with his wife Samantha looking on. The nation had been hoping for reassurance, soothing words from a seasoned politician who had guided the Ship of State for six years: that is not what they got. Although he had previously hinted that he would continue as prime minister whatever the outcome, Cameron clearly felt that he could not stay on in the circumstances. It was not obvious when he began to speak that he was about to resign but as he started to list his achievements, including the introduction of gay marriage, an issue that was so contentious it had pushed many previous Conservative Party supporters into the arms of the UK Independence Party (UKIP) and thus towards divorce from the EU, the reality of the situation became clear. In the weeks to come many who ticked 'Leave' on the ballot paper complained that they had merely been registering a protest vote, but they were sharply disabused of this as the PM fell.

David Cameron was certainly at his eloquent best. 'I held nothing back, I was absolutely clear about my belief that Britain is stronger, safer and better off inside the European Union and I made clear the referendum was about this and this alone – not the future of any single politician, including myself,' he said, his voice beginning to tremble with emotion. In the background Samantha's look of concern was growing and as his words began to register with listeners, there was yet another shockwave as the full implications of the Brexit vote started to become clear.

'But the British people have made a very clear decision to take a different path and as such, I think the country requires fresh leadership to take it in this direction,' Mr Cameron continued. 'I will do everything I can as Prime Minister to steady the ship over the coming weeks and months but I do not think it would be right for me to try to be the captain that steers our country to its next destination. This is not a decision I've taken lightly but I do believe it's in the national interest to have a period of stability and then the new leadership required.'

There were words of reassurance – Her Majesty the Queen would be kept informed, the Governor of the Bank of England, Mark Carney, OC, would make a statement – but there was no disguising the enormity of what had happened. The thorny issue of the EU had just claimed the scalp of yet another Conservative prime minister, the third in a row to have fallen beneath the wheels of the Brussels juggernaut. Who would replace him? What would happen next? And above all, when would the UK formally invoke Article 50, the means by which a country leaves the EU? David Cameron was adamant he was not going to do it, and although the story circulated at the time that he saw no reason to do all the hard negotiating work and allow the likes of Boris Johnson to claim the glory, it is equally plausible that he did not want to go down in history as the man who started the process that would lead to a constitutional earthquake. Although having been the man who resolved to hold the referendum in the first place, despite a good deal of advice to do no such thing, it was perhaps a little late to worry about that.

The week that followed would have taxed the ingenuity of a thriller writer, for no author of fiction could have competed with the facts. For a start, on that initial weekend, as the world continued to turn on its axis and yet there was a clear sense that a new order was about to emerge, almost every senior politician in the UK seemed to go to ground. Britain's Chancellor of the Exchequer, George Osborne, author of the so-called 'Project Fear' designed to keep Britain in the EU, appeared to vanish without trace. More to the point, so too did the Tory clown prince in waiting, Boris Johnson, and his acolyte, the Lord Chancellor and Secretary of State for Justice, Michael Gove. Indeed, the two men, who more than anyone had been responsible for the outcome of the referendum, appeared to have been terrified by what they had done. There was no grandstanding for the simple reason that there was no anything from either of them: they appeared to be as shocked as anyone else. When they were finally spotted, they resembled nothing so much as frightened mice. Nor was there any semblance of public rejoicing or indeed triumphalism from much of the Leave campaign, which seemed as stunned by the gravity of the situation as anyone else.

It was to be several days before anyone rallied, as incredulity from the rest of the world began to sink in. The Prime Minister had declared that his replacement should be in place by the Conservative Party Conference in October 2016 and it was expected that the process to choose the next Tory leader would take about two months. It was also anticipated that the crown would be handed to the charismatic Boris Johnson. Long beloved of the grass roots, Johnson was unusual in that his appeal stretched out much further than to the Conservative party faithful: he was the Tory, it was said, who could reach parts no other Tory could reach. He had been the de facto leader of the Leave campaign, fractious and disunited as it had been, and as such surely he would be the person to lead the UK into the bright new future he had been forecasting. Or would he? Doubts were voiced from the start.

Boris Johnson was undoubtedly a good journalist, a great one even, and as Mayor of London he had been efficient and successful, not least in winning the mayorship in a Labour city – but was he really up to the job? As mayor, he was said to delegate a great deal, never paying much attention to detail. In the House of Commons, where he was now an MP, he hadn't built up his own group of backers. Tellingly, he was not especially popular among his fellow elected representatives. There were doubts as to his moral compass too – he was known to have had a string of extra-marital affairs and had sired at least one love child. Above all there was the ongoing suspicion that his play-act of bumbling incompetence masked the reality that he really was a bumbling incompetent and if ever Britain needed a safe pair of hands, it was now.

But Boris did have one unique selling point and that was Michael Gove. Blinking owlishly behind his glasses, Gove, who had repeatedly ruled himself out as a contender for the leadership, had carved out a reputation as one of the party's thinkers, and if this cerebral and principled man was backing Johnson, the thinking went, then surely Boris could not be the liability some feared. It all boiled down to this: the charismatic one lacked the necessary experience while the experienced one lacked any charisma. But in this brave new world of British politics, perhaps it could be made to work?

For all the fact that the two had led the Leave campaign and that Boris's undoubted popularity was a significant factor in what would come next, no one could say there was a great deal of enthusiasm at the idea of a Prime Minister Johnson. Meanwhile, the situation in the rest of the country was turning quite febrile. Just a few hours after the announcement of the result of the referendum, a petition was launched calling for a second one, on the grounds that the result was secured on less than 60 per cent of the vote on a turnout of less than 75 per cent. Ironically, this petition was actually launched by a Leave enthusiast, William Oliver Healey, before the referendum had been held. Healey distanced himself from the petition, which was now being called for by those who wanted to Remain and initially it did seem that it would have some effect: ultimately it garnered more than four million signatures, which meant it had to be debated in Parliament. But it soon became clear that this was clutching at straws, with the Prime Minister stating firmly, it was 'not remotely on the cards'.

Meanwhile, on the other side of the political ring, there was a growing sense of panic from the left. The lame duck Labour leader Jeremy Corbyn, who was popular with Labour

Party activists but generally despised by his MPs, was widely perceived to have totally failed in his duty to help the Remain vote. While publicly calling for the UK to stay in the EU, it was widely believed that Corbyn's sympathies actually lay with the Leavers, and certainly his performance, even by his own low standards, had been lamentable. Utterly incapable of inspiring any sort of passion or loyalty from his own MPs and kept in place only by the fact that his predecessor Ed Miliband's disastrous decision to lower the price of party membership to £3 had allowed in a ragtag mixture of the sort of extreme Trotskyite sympathisers the party had battled to rid itself of three decades earlier, who saw in Jeremy their champion, Corbyn came across as a student union activist utterly out of his depth in a situation of national crisis. Nor was he even proving a rallying point on the left. While moderate Labour members looked on in abject despair as their party leapt into the political abyss, even erstwhile supporters, furious that he had betrayed them over the EU, began to turn away. They were caught in a seemingly intractable bind: there was no way they could force Corbyn out while he had such widespread support among party members and yet he was leading them into political oblivion. How much worse could it get?

With the two main parties in such a state of turmoil, a prime minister who had effectively lost his powerbase the moment he announced his resignation and a leader of the opposition who was shortly and publicly about to be renounced by 80 per cent of his MPs, added to which was all the uncertainty about what was to happen after the Brexit vote, the UK was in a state of political paralysis, with a void at the heart of government that was potentially dangerous. It was extremely instructive to watch what the Conservative Party, often called the most efficient vote-winning machine in history, and the Labour Party, which had never attracted that epithet, did next.

By 29 June, the day on which nominations closed, there were two clear front runners: Boris Johnson and Home Secretary Theresa May. She had played her hand extremely cannily during the run-up to the referendum: although she allowed it to be known that she was a reluctant supporter of Remain, she had maintained a very low profile during the campaign. While that stance had garnered criticism from some quarters, it did mean that she had stayed out of the personal and bitter infighting that had characterised so much of the proceedings. Some people felt that in the wake of the result of the referendum, the next PM should be a Leaver – that was certainly the view of Boris Johnson's supporters – but the wiser heads knew that what was really called for was a unity candidate. And there was no one better placed than Mrs May to command that. Meanwhile, the charismatic Boris looked set to clean up: the party faithful loved him, he was one of the Tory Big Beasts – and if truth be told, given that he had almost certainly played a huge role in the outcome of the referendum, he had a moral duty, in the eyes of many, to get on with clearing up the mess. Boris pulled ahead at the beginning but later polls had Theresa catching him up. Indeed, the race was neck and neck.

On Thursday, 30 June, just one week after the referendum that had changed British politics, and dressed in a tartan trouser suit – a nod, it was said, to placate Scotland, which had voted to Remain – Theresa May stepped up to the podium. 'My pitch is very simple. I'm Theresa May and I think I'm the best person to be prime minister,' she began. There followed a list of promises: Brexit would mean Brexit, there would be no snap election or emergency budget (one of Chancellor of the Exchequer George Osborne's threats), there would be no change to the status of EU nationals living in Britain and vice versa, and social justice would be at the forefront of everything she did.

'I know I'm not a showy politician,' Mrs May continued. 'I don't tour the television studios. I don't gossip about people over lunch. I don't go drinking in Parliament's bars. I don't often wear my heart on my sleeve. I just get on with the job in front of me. And you can judge me by my record. As Home Secretary, I was told I couldn't take on the Police Federation, but I did. I was told I couldn't cut police spending without crime going up, but crime is lower than ever. I was told I shouldn't start asking questions about police corruption, but everywhere I've seen it – from Stephen Lawrence to Hillsborough – I've exposed it. I was told I couldn't stop Gary McKinnon's extradition, but I stood up to the American government and I stopped it. I was told I couldn't deport Abu

Qatada, but I flew to Jordan and negotiated the treaty that got him out of Britain for good.'

Meanwhile, in the Boris Johnson camp, there was uproar at an extraordinary and totally out-of-character betrayal at the heart of the campaign, which was to destroy his chances for good. With just three hours to go before the nominations closed, Michael Gove, who was also to destroy himself in the process, quite suddenly announced that he was withdrawing his backing from Boris and intended to stand himself. 'Boris is a big character with great abilities and I enjoyed working with him in the referendum campaign, when he campaigned with great energy and enthusiasm,' he said. 'But there is something special about leading a party and leading a country, and I had the opportunity in the last few days to assess whether or not Boris could lead that team and build that unity. And I came reluctantly but firmly to the conclusion that while Boris has many talents and attributes, he wasn't capable of building that team. And there were a number of people who had said to me during the course of the week, "Michael, it should be you".'

This statement provoked utter astonishment from all sides. For a start, Gove and Johnson, who had both started out as journalists, had known each other for about thirty years, and so it was widely perceived that it was a little late in the day for Michael suddenly to wake up to Boris's character flaws. Many saw the hand of Gove's wife, the journalist Sarah Vine, as being behind this: in a recent piece for the *Daily Mail*, where she had a weekly column as one the media's 'Wednesday witches', she had, post-referendum, written that 'he – we – are now charged with implementing the instructions of 17 million people,' prompting widespread derision on the basis that she was not actually an elected representative of the people.

She had then followed up with an email to her husband and several aides that was leaked:

> Very important that we focus now on the individual obstacles and thoroughly overcome them before moving to the next. I really think Michael needs to have a Henry or a Beth [Gove's special advisers]with him for this morning's critical meetings.
>
> One simple message you MUST have SPECIFIC assurances from Boris OTHERWISE you cannot guarantee your support.
>
> The details can be worked out later on, but without that you have no leverage.
>
> Crucially the membership will not have the necessary reassurance to back Boris, neither will Dacre/Murdoch, who instinctively dislike Boris but trust your ability enough to support a Boris/Gove ticket.
>
> Do not concede any ground. Be your stubborn best.
> GOOD LUCK

The Dacre referred to, of course, was none other than Paul Dacre, editor of the *Daily Mail* and thus Sarah Vine's boss.

He was also notoriously averse to any personal publicity and all manner of trouble was forecast for Vine, who had emerged looking shallow, foolish and out of her depth: 'Lady Macbeth without the charm' was one verdict.

Another rumour is that George Osborne, well known to be a practitioner of the Machiavellian arts, had put him up to it. The two men were friends and were known to have continued to meet quietly behind the scenes, including a session at Dorneywood, the Chancellor's grace-and-favour country house, two weeks previously; and although Osborne, until a short period beforehand, had looked to be one of the strongest contenders to succeed David Cameron, those hopes had been shattered, almost certainly for good. However, it was conceivable that were Gove able to rally the Leavers behind him, then he could take over as leader, with Osborne staying on as Chancellor, or possibly moving to the Foreign Office. In any case, the plot was to come spectacularly unstuck.

Whatever anyone's view of Michael Gove, he had a reputation for decency and integrity and to behave in such an extraordinary manner was not only perplexing, but added another couple of bodies to the growing pile of victims taken down by events – first, Boris's and then his own. His actions were widely met with disdain: this was the sort of childish student politics that had no place on the world stage, especially at a time of cataclysmic change, was the verdict. But he certainly finished Boris's leadership ambitions off. A week after watching his old school friend and rival David Cameron fall on his sword, Johnson was forced to do likewise and like the PM it was not immediately obvious what he was going to do. After spending 11 minutes listing all his own numerous achievements along with the challenges that lay ahead, the blond bombshell went on to drop a bombshell of his own: 'That is the agenda for the next prime minister of this country. My friends, you have waited for the punchline for this speech,' he said. 'That having consulted colleagues and in view of the circumstances in Parliament, I have concluded that person cannot be me.'

The reaction from all quarters was one of astonishment – and fury. 'I think there will be a profound sense of dismay and, frankly, contempt,' observed Michael, now Lord, Heseltine, a member of Margaret Thatcher's government and himself no stranger to political treachery. 'He's ripped the party apart. He's created the greatest constitutional crisis of modern times. He's knocked billions off the value of the nation's savings. He's like a general that led his army to the sound of guns and at the sight of the battlefield, abandoned the field – to the claims of his adjutant, who said he wasn't up to the job in the first place. I've never seen so contemptible and irresponsible a situation. It's a free society. There's no question of punishment. He must live with the shame of what he's done.'

The headline writers competed with each other to express the greatest shock: 'Brexecuted,' roared *The Sun*. 'Tory day of treachery,' shrieked *The Mail*, losing no time in doing what it always did and backing a winner – 'A party in flames and why it *must* be Theresa.' 'An act of midnight treachery,' opined the *Daily Telegraph*. And so it went on. Boris's father, journalist, author and environmentalist Stanley Johnson, made his own feelings towards his son's assassin known: '"*Et tu, Brute*" is my comment,' he observed. 'I don't think he is called Brutus, but you never know.'

There was real anger at Johnson at the outset, the feeling being that, given he had brought the nation to such a pretty pass, the least he could do was play a part in solving the crisis, and less fury at Gove, but as time passed and the full implications began to sink in of what the Secretary of State for Justice had done, the mood began to change. But one element that did not change was that after Gove stabbed Boris in the back, the front and the side, and as soon as Boris had finished off the job by putting himself out of his misery, Theresa May drew ahead in the race and did not look back. By the time the dust settled at the end of the day, there were five contenders: Theresa May, Michael Gove, former Defence Secretary Liam Fox, Work and Pensions Secretary Stephen Crabb and Minister of State (Department of Energy and Climate Change) Andrea Leadsom. The latter two were not at all well known to the wider public, although an early indication that Gove's machinations were about to blow up in his face came when a number of high-profile Leave MPs, including Boris himself and Bernard Jenkin, threw their support behind Leadsom and not Michael Gove.

At the time it appeared that the Conservative Party continued in chaos, with the leadership election set to chunter on in all its bad-tempered turmoil until the autumn of that year, although very shortly afterwards it became clear that this was the moment when the Tories began to focus, reassemble and get on with their recovery, the political vote-winning machine getting back on the road again. Meanwhile Labour continued to tear itself apart with votes of no confidence in the leader Jeremy Corbyn, and mass resignations among the Shadow Cabinet as the Tories regrouped and began to get on with the job in hand.

On the first ballot, held on 5 July, Mrs May came a clear first with half the votes of the parliamentary party, 165 representing 50.2 per cent; slightly more surprisingly Andrea Leadsom came second, with 66 votes representing 20.1 per cent. Michael Gove was a poor third, with 43 votes (14.6 per cent), while Liam Fox came last and so was knocked out of the race. Stephen Crabb – a somewhat controversial figure due to remarks that had been attributed to him and that he later denied, to the effect that homosexuality was 'curable' – clearly realised he didn't stand a chance and so dropped out himself.

The second ballot was held two days later: Mrs May, now very clearly set to win, polled 199 votes (60.5 per cent of the vote), with Mrs Leadsom gaining 84 votes (25.5 per cent) and Mr Gove, now clearly a badly damaged figure, gaining just 46 votes or 14 per cent of the total. He too was eliminated from the race. It was down to the last two to fight it out and for the first time ever the contenders were both women; even more excitingly for the spectator was that neither was there because of tokenism (the Conservatives had wisely avoided implementing all-women shortlists, which had produced such a crowd of mediocrities in the Labour Party) but because both were spectacularly well qualified for the job. Labour moderates could only look on in disbelief and envy: the Conservatives were about to elect their second female prime minister while the so-called party of equality and opportunity was now dominated by a bunch of dinosaurs with any female Labour MPs who dared to speak out threatened with violence and intimidation. Not that any but the Westminster village and its dwindling band of supporters cared much about Labour: the real race was going on elsewhere.

Andrea Leadsom was in fact something of an unknown quantity: with a solid background in the financial sector, she had entered Parliament in 2010 and began working her way up the greasy pole, first in the Treasury and more recently in the Department of Energy and Climate Change. Initially a proponent of Remain, her views had changed over years in government and she played a prominent and well-respected role in the referendum, appearing in the BBC *Great Debate* alongside Boris Johnson and the Labour MP Gisela Stuart on the Leave panel. It was generally held that she had had a good war.

But problems arose almost immediately in her campaign.

For a start, she showed some reluctance to publish her tax returns, following an example set by David Cameron when his late father, Ian Cameron, was implicated in the Panama Papers scandal in April 2016, saying that she would do so if she made the final ballot. In the event she published one year's worth of financial information against Mrs May, who revealed four years of returns. There were claims in some quarters that what she had published was not actually a tax return, merely some information, and while there was no question whatsoever that anyone alleged any wrongdoing, there was a concern in some quarters that Mrs Leadsom and her husband Ben, who owned a buy-to-let business, might have managed their affairs in a very tax-efficient way. There were other rumblings, too, with some allegations that Leadsom had embellished her CV, making her City career look more impressive than it actually was.

Far worse, however, far, far worse, was the row that had broken out about childlessness. It was well known that Theresa May and her husband Philip did not have children; several years previously Theresa hinted at the pain it had caused them and in the run-up to the leadership vote proper, had given an interview to the *Daily Mail* in which she talked about the deep sadness she and her husband both felt. That being the case, it was a case of naivety at best, crassness and cruelty at worst, and spectacular ineptitude whatever the case, but Andrea Leadsom totally destroyed her own leadership bid when she gave an interview to *The Times* which implied that as a mother, she was better suited to the role. Under the headline, 'Being a mother gives me edge on May – Leadsom', the newspaper quoted her as saying Mrs May 'possibly has nieces, nephews, lots of people. But I have children who are going to have children, who will directly be part of what happens next.'

The ensuing uproar had Leadsom reading a statement outside her home in Northamptonshire, saying she was 'disgusted about how this has been presented. In the course of a lengthy interview yesterday, I was repeatedly asked about my children and I repeatedly made it clear that I did not want this in any way a feature of the campaign.' *The Times* responded by publishing a tape of the interview that made it clear that this was exactly what she had said.

Another row erupted with accusations that Leadsom herself had been the victim of a dirty-tricks campaign that would stop at nothing to destroy her but the damage had been well and truly done and there were still another couple of months of this to run. And then, in another spectacular display of the Tories exercising the self-discipline they so often showed in moments of crisis, Mrs Leadsom, having already apologised to Mrs May, decided to lay down her political life (only briefly, as it emerged) for the sake of her party. On 11 July, she withdrew from the race: 'Strong leadership is needed urgently to begin the work of withdrawing from the European Union. A nine-week leadership campaign at such a critical moment is highly undesirable,' she began in a short statement. Theresa May was 'ideally placed to implement Brexit on the best possible terms for the British people and she has promised she will do so. I have however concluded that the interests of our country are best served by the immediate appointment of a strong and well-supported prime minister. I am therefore withdrawing from the leadership election, and I wish Mrs May the very greatest success.'

And so it was done. In an astonishing reshaping of the political landscape in just a few weeks, a revolution of sorts had taken place. An urbane Old Etonian prime minister and his similarly privileged band of cohorts had gone, to be replaced by a grammar school girl who was not so much the Iron Lady that Margaret Thatcher had been as, according to her erstwhile Cabinet colleague Nick Clegg, an Ice Queen. And the sense of relief was palpable: Theresa May may not be the most flamboyant of politicians, but she exuded caution and common sense, exactly the two qualities needed at a time of national crisis. But while a great deal was known about her professional life, almost nothing was about her personal life.

So who was she, this unassuming woman with a taste for racy kitten heels, who had unseated the established order and ended up at the top of the top table? Who was the newly elected PM?

2

UPSTAIRS, DOWNSTAIRS

In the early years of the twenty-first century, the exclusive west London enclave of Notting Hill came to be associated with a very patrician type of Tory. David Cameron lived in the area, as did George Osborne and Michael Gove. Notting Hill exudes wealth: expensive shops stand on what were once the sites of scrap-metal yards, trendy cafés rub shoulders with Michelin-starred restaurants and yummy mummies trot from yoga classes to vegan restaurants by way of some very exclusive health clubs. We might have been all in it together, according to the recently ousted Tory grandees, but some were more in it than most.

Over a century earlier, however, although parts of the area were wealthy, it was very different from the urbane and privileged clique of sophisticated chic it would later become.

The huge stucco-fronted white houses belonged to a world that no longer exists, one of sharp class divides that it was not so easy to bridge, but also one in which middle-class families lived in grand houses looked after by a raft of staff in the kind of lifestyle only the extremely wealthy would be able to afford today.

Caroline Henderson was typical of these: a sixty-five-year-old widow from Liverpool in 1901, she lived in one such house on Lansdowne Road with her two single daughters, aged thirty-six and twenty-nine, looked after by four members of staff. Surrounded by large communal gardens and a short walk away from leafy Holland Park, it was a peaceful and attractive area in which to live, whether you were upstairs or downstairs. And at that time most large dwellings housed both.

A census was carried out in 1901 that revealed this information and the journalist Roy Stockdill, with a strong interest in genealogy, was the first to delve into the details it gave of Theresa May's forebears, to flesh out the background of the then Home Secretary as interest in her began to grow and as it became increasingly apparent that she was going to become one of the political greats. The domestic staff at 40 Lansdowne Road, however, would not have been able to conceive of such a thing, for, back then, the idea of anyone, especially a woman – women didn't even have the vote at that point – rising from this background to give birth to the father of a future prime minister would have been risible.

One of those living downstairs at the turn of the last century was Amy Patterson, a parlour maid who was twenty-two in 1901. In later years she was known as 'Granny Amy' by her granddaughter, Britain's second female prime minister, and her relatively humble origins, which are mirrored on the maternal side of the family, go a long way towards explaining the disdain Mrs May sometimes seemed to show towards the public-school-educated elite who preceded her, with their aristocratic forebears and inherited wealth, and why she acted so fast to replace them with a Cabinet that stemmed mainly from humbler origins, in her case with both sides of her family descended from domestic staff. She knew both her grandmothers and although her father had started the journey out of the working class that so many people were to make in the middle of the twentieth century, the young Theresa would have known that the privileged elite were looked after by a considerably less privileged army of servants, with the Britain of 1901 seeing 1.5 million people working as servants, more than were employed in agriculture or in mining, at that time a huge employer of working-class men.

Not that her grandmother worked in one of the large country houses with an army of staff behind the green baize doors that was as strictly regimented, according to domestic position, as the inhabitants upstairs: this was a much smaller set-up, although with modern appliances still unknown, it would have been a life of hard work. Amy Margaret Patterson was born in 1878, in Plaistow, Essex, to a butler called David Patterson (or Paterson), who was born in 1852.

David also came from a background of backbreaking hard work: his father was a labourer called Alexander, who had married Margaret Watson. Born in a former mining village called Kennet in Clackmannshire on the banks of the River Forth, David moved to Glasgow, where in 1875 he married the London-born Jane Poole. The couple then relocated to Wimbledon, an affluent suburb of south London, where David found work as a butler, before dying in 1893 at the young age of forty-two. The couple had three children: Amy, her older sister Lottie and little brother David, Theresa May's paternal great-aunt and uncle.

Although this was not an age widely associated with travel, various family members saw far more of the world than might be expected, not least because Britain at that time still had a mighty empire and it was common for many people, whatever their class background, to work in various areas of it. Amy was one of them. As a teenager, she was sent by her father to work for a family in Christchurch, New Zealand, but became homesick and after two years she came home, a long journey to be taken by sea, lasting forty days and on ships that were also arranged on a class basis, with wealthy passengers travelling cabin and the less rich downstairs, as it were, in steerage. No documentary evidence exists as to how Amy travelled, but it would almost certainly have been in steerage, where travellers would sleep on rows of bunks divided between single men, single women (who would have been protected by the crew from unwanted attention) and married couples.

People were able to socialise more freely during the day, however, passing their time watching the mysteries of the ocean unfurl before them, playing deck games and attending church services, which were not as rigidly broken down on class lines. Amy would have experienced this on both voyages but on the journey back there turned out to be a quite different kind of diversion when she met her future husband, a soldier called Tom Brasier. These were more moralistic times and the relationship would not have progressed far, but it proved to be the foundation for the course of most of Amy's life. Tom disembarked in India and Amy sailed on to Southampton, but the two kept in touch, corresponding regularly.

When Amy returned to the UK, she took up residence in the Henderson establishment in Lansdowne Road, Notting Hill. As a parlour maid she would probably not have had to perform the heaviest duties such as scouring the grate and cleaning the carpet, very hard labour in those pre-hoover days – the housemaid would typically perform those – but even so, her life would have been much harder than any lived today and that for an annual wage of about £18–£30 (in today's terms, roughly £6,500–£10,700). She would have been expected to get up early to make sure the house was in order, wear a uniform and do lighter chores such as polishing and dusting and answering the door to visitors, whom she would then announce, as well as waiting on the family at mealtimes.

That uniform would almost certainly have changed in the

course of the day: typically in the morning parlour maids wore a print dress, set off with a white cap and an apron, and then in the afternoon they would change into a black dress with a white collar and cuffs, a smart muslin cap and an apron. Amy would never have worn jewellery when on duty and she would have been expected to glide around noiselessly in the background. There were many manuals about Victorian household management, the most famous published from 1861 onwards in instalments by Mrs Isabella Beeton, and it is stressed that the appearance of a parlour maid should be neat and simple and her demeanour quiet and dignified.

Amy would have been responsible for keeping the rooms in the house in good order, arranging flowers and writing materials, and if there was no lady's maid, helping Mrs Henderson and her daughters with their dress. In her spare time, of which there would not have been much, she would have been expected to mend clothes, tidy and, at the end of the day, lock up the house and deal with the lights. A parlour maid's hours were typically 6.30 a.m. to 10.30 p.m. but for all that, if a person was lucky enough to find herself in a decent household, it was a better life than most could have been expected to live outside. Amy would have received board and lodging in a large house in a good area, although she would have had limited time off.

She clearly used it to keep in touch with her soldier, for eight years later, when Amy was thirty-one and Tom twenty-nine, they married in the Independent Chapel, Fareham,

Hampshire, on 25 September 1909. It's not clear what took them so long, as thirty-one was a very late age for a woman to marry back then, but it is possible that Tom wished to ensure that he had the means to keep his family properly, as his background was no more elevated than hers, and Amy did indeed give up her work as a parlour maid and devote herself to looking after her family from then on.

Tom Brasier did not come from a domestic service background: rather, he came from a family of carpenters and builders that was based in Limpsfield, Surrey, and had been working at that trade for generations, possibly as far back as the seventeenth century; there is even a house called Brasier's Cottage in Limpsfield. His parents, James and Sarah Jane, had married in 1865 in Lewes, Sussex: James was a carpenter, born to another carpenter, Richard, and his wife Ann. His eldest son, also called Richard, followed him into the profession.

Tom was born to James and Sarah Jane in 1880 in Wimbledon, south London, the fifth of eight siblings. Unlike his elder brother Richard, he did not wish to follow his father into the building trade. Tom had other ideas: he wanted to join the army and as such, like his future bride, he was also to see a bit of the wider world. He decided to join the King's Royal Rifles, an infantry rifle regiment of the British Army, which dated back to 1756, when it was raised to defend thirteen colonies in what is now the United States against the French and Native American forces and also saw action in the Napoleonic Wars. It took the name it had when Tom joined in 1830.

It is entirely possible that Tom fought in the Second Boer War in South Africa, which lasted from 1899 to 1902, because his regiment played a key role in the first battle at Talana Hill, but there is no historical confirmation of this. But the army played a crucial role in the nation's life: this was a time when the British Empire stretched across the globe and the army was deployed to keep it under control. Whether or not Tom served in South Africa, he certainly did in India, and after marrying Amy, he was sent back to India and his new wife followed him, where she bore him two sons, one of whom died in infancy.

Tom rose to become a sergeant-major in the King's Royal Rifles and the family returned to the UK and London, where Amy gave birth to three more children, including, on 20 August 1917, Hubert, Theresa's father. He was born during World War I while Tom was away fighting, which he did with gallantry and was decorated. After the war he became a clerk. He eventually died in 1951 at the age of seventy-one.

'I remember her [Amy] as an old lady in a wheelchair who bore her problems well,' said Theresa's paternal cousin Alan Brasier, sixty-nine, a former textile firm executive living in Gloucester, in an interview with the *Daily Mail* in 2015. 'She was kind and honest, a straightforward person who knew her own mind. And she was the type who would not tell anyone if she was feeling poorly; you had to worm it out of her' – in other words, much like her granddaughter, who is not given to public complaint.

But it was the next generation that began to mark a clear change in circumstance, breaking out of the working class and into a very different sphere. Theresa's father Hubert trained as a man of the cloth at the College of the Resurrection at Mirfield, West Yorkshire, signalling a clear step up the social ladder (although he would have seen his move as following a vocation, not a way of stepping up in the world), away from labouring and the army and into a solid middle-class lifestyle. This was a time when the old class structures of Britain were beginning to break down, while increased opportunities in education were giving bright children from poorer backgrounds the chance to shine, as was to happen with Theresa herself.

Meanwhile, other family members were also breaking away from their working-class background as so many did at the time, taking full advantage of Britain's increasingly egalitarian culture, one which was to allow not one but two women to rise from a humble background and achieve the highest office in the land. Academia was to be the field in which other family members would excel, with three of Amy and Tom's grandchildren becoming professors: they included Professor Martin Brasier, who was at Oxford University. One of the world's leading experts in microfossils, he tragically perished in a car crash just before Christmas 2014. The others are Clive Brasier, an expert on tree diseases, who is visiting professor at Imperial College and emeritus mycologist with the Forestry Commission, as well as serving at one point as a governmental adviser on forestry, and finally Andrew Parrott, professor of psychology at Swansea University and an authority on the effects of recreational drugs on the brain. All would have known of their grandparents' relatively humble roots; all would end up in very different positions from their origins.

Professor Parrott remembers his grandmother: 'After she was widowed, she lived with us at my parents' house in Surrey for several years while I was at school,' he told the *Daily Mail*. in February 2015. 'She would listen to the BBC Home Service with an earphone rigged up by my father and knit woollen squares to send to Africa and other poor areas. She was always sending off cheques as well, though she didn't have much money of her own. But she cared. And she was always interested in what we were doing at school. So lively, and very proud of the family.'

Eventually Amy went to live in a nursing home in Oxford, where she died, aged eighty-eight, in 1967.

Mrs May's mother also comes from a family of domestic staff, although in her case the circumstances are slightly different. Theresa's maternal grandmother was called Violet Jenny Welland (later 'Grannie Vie', although she insisted on being called 'Grandma') and she was born in Plymouth, Devon, in 1894 to William, a store porter. The family moved to Reading, Berkshire, and in her teens Violet went to work for an Australian astronomer, Walter Duffield, and his wife Doris as a nursery nurse for their eleven-month-old daughter, Joan.

The Duffields were later to return to Australia, where Walter established the country's first observatory on Mount Stromlo near Canberra before dying in 1929. While still in the UK, they lived in Reading, in a large red-brick house, as grand as Lansdowne Road, but 40 miles outside London, and it was while working for them that Violet met Reginald Barnes, a leather worker and salesman from Milton, Hampshire, whose primary business was making shoes (an interest that clearly reappeared in his granddaughter). Just five feet tall and a lithe and slender young woman, Violet caught his eye immediately. Even in old age her vivacity was apparent: 'Grannie was quite a force,' said Glenys Barnes, who married Theresa's cousin Adrian, on the other side of the family, an aircraft systems safety engineer. Speaking to the *Daily Mail* in February 2015, she added, 'She was a tiny lady, but very positive, very determined and very, very forceful.'

The two started courting in the innocent way that was prevalent back then, with a clear sign that marriage was on the cards. World War I got in the way of the budding romance, however, and Reg was sent off as a private in the Army Service Corps to serve in the East Africa campaign. Violet gave him a photo of herself to comfort him during their separation: on the back she wrote, 'To Reg from Vie with fondest and truest with all good wishes for great success in East Africa. The ocean between lies such a distance be our lot/Should thou never see me? Love: forget me not.'

Very many women of that generation saw their husbands

or fiancés killed in the war, of course, and were destined never to marry, with three-quarters of a million men killed and many more incapacitated. But this particular couple was luckier than so many whose dreams and future were destroyed in the Great War. Reg survived and returned to marry the twenty-four-year-old Violet in Reading in 1917, the same year that Theresa's father, Hubert, was born. But Violet went on to suffer further tragedy as the 1918 outbreak of Spanish flu killed both her father William and a brother, a horrible irony for so many as they had managed to survive the war only to succumb to a flu epidemic that killed so many more.

Families pulled together in those days: there was no social security and not a great deal else and so in the wake of those sad deaths Violet and Reg moved in with her widowed mother in Southampton Street, Reading. There wasn't a great deal of space in which the extended family could live: home was a small house with an outside loo and trams running right outside the front door, and an aunt was also resident. The contrast with the country estates and town mansions of the Tory grandees whom Theresa May later replaced could scarcely have been more marked, and must have made a direct impression on her world view and understanding about those who were not born with a silver spoon in their mouth. Violet remained there for much of her life.

Like Amy, Violet was quite old for the time when she started a family and it is not clear why: she was thirty when she gave birth to Maurice in 1924, with Zaidee Mary, Mrs May's mother, arriving four years later. After Theresa started to become better known and interest in her background grew, some people wondered whether her unusual name meant the family were Jewish or had links to the Middle East, but the truth is somewhat more prosaic. Violet chose the name of their son and her husband Reg that of their daughter, and as a committed Christian (like Theresa), he almost certainly picked it because it's the name of Abraham's wife in the Old Testament. There were strongly Christian values on both sides of the family: Hubert, of course, was to become a vicar, but Zaidee also came from a religious background and faith was as important to her as it was going to be to her daughter. Just as modest beginnings played a strong role in moulding the young Theresa, so, too, did the Christian faith.

But the family did have ordeals to cope with: in Violet's later years complications after a smallpox vaccination put her into a wheelchair, where she remained for the rest of her life. There were similarities with the other set of grandparents, too, as in both cases the women were widowed for some considerable period of time. Reg died, aged seventy-eight, in 1970 and Violet did likewise eighteen years later at the age of ninety-four.

This, then, is the background that shaped Theresa May. There was nothing flashy or showy about it. At the turn of the last century, both sets of grandparents came from solid working-class stock and the families began to better their circumstances through hard work and increased opportunity. They grew up in a world that is long gone, however: a world in which Britain ruled a third of the globe through her empire, where church-going was the norm, where flamboyance was frowned on (in some circles, at least), and a world about to go through cataclysmic change. Both of Theresa's grandfathers fought in World War I and she was born in the aftermath of World War II, a conflict that would alter the world order and radically revise Britain's relationship with the rest of the globe.

But there would be much that would benefit people, too. Until the last few decades of the twentieth century, Britain had an education system that was not only the envy of the world but directly enabled clever children from less privileged backgrounds to go on and make something of their lives. Theresa herself benefited from that, of which more in the next chapter. There was a great deal more that was about to change, as well. In 1918 women over the age of thirty finally got the vote and a decade later, thanks to the Equal Franchise Act, they attained voting equality with men. In 1919 Nancy Astor became the first female MP to take her seat and for the first time in British history (if you don't count the monarchy) a career in politics opened up to women.

It is sometimes said that World War I spelled an end to the age of luxury and a beginning to that of comfort: Theresa May's family might not have had the luxury (they were, in modern parlance, the 'ennablers' of it for other people), but they certainly benefited from the comfort as it became the norm for every family to have refrigerators and washing machines, cars and vacuum cleaners, televisions, foreign holidays and opportunity. With the introduction of domestic conveniences the age of drudgery was over. The women of the twentieth century who hold similar positions to those of Theresa May's forebears will have a far easier time of it than they would have done just over a century ago.

But while she might have achieved the highest office in the land, Theresa has never forgotten where she came from, the rigours and privations endured by her grandparents and the dutiful nature she took on from her parents when she was just a child. Given that her first six years in government were spent under a patrician, Old Etonian prime minister, it came as quite a shock to some when she made it obvious from the moment she took office that hers was to be a very different kind of Conservative government, one that spoke directly to the people from whence she came.

Her inaugural speech when she became prime minister might have been directed at her grandparents just as much as at modern-day Britain, to whom she positioned herself as an inclusive, traditional one-nation Tory: 'If you're from an ordinary working-class family, life is much harder than many people in Westminster realise,' she told the nation as she addressed them for the first time in her new role. 'You have a job, but you don't always have job security. You have your own home but you worry about paying the mortgage.

You can just about manage, but you worry about the cost of living and getting your kids into a good school.

'If you are one of those families, if you're just managing, I want to address you directly. I know you are working around the clock, I know you're doing your best and I know that sometimes life can be a struggle. The government I lead will be driven, not by the interests of the privileged few but by yours. We will do everything we can to give you more control over your lives. When we take the big calls we will think not of the powerful, but you. When we pass new laws we will listen not to the mighty, but to you.'

If it was her grandparents who informed her knowledge about the struggle to improve oneself in Britain today, then it was her parents who nurtured and formed her, from a dutiful and hardworking schoolgirl into one of the most powerful women in the world.

3

THE VICAR'S DAUGHTER

By the 1950s, Britain was a totally different country from the one it had been half a century earlier, when Theresa May's grandparents were coming into their prime. World War II was over, with its bloody battles, the horror and the terror of the Holocaust and the fact that just two decades after the cataclysmic events of World War I, Europe had torn itself into shreds again. Germany had been split in two, into the democratic West Germany and the communist East Germany, and the Cold War was under way, but it was the last war, the global war, which had shattered generations. In the Chancelleries and the seats of government across the Continent, Europe's leaders were uniting in one goal: this must not happen again.

Indeed, plans were already afoot to stop Europe and

specifically France and Germany from entering into such catastrophic conflict again. In 1951, the European Coal and Steel Community (ECSC) was established following the Treaty of Paris. France, West Germany, Belgium, Italy, the Netherlands and Luxembourg all signed up. It was the brainchild of French Foreign Minister Robert Schuman: the aim was to 'make war not only unthinkable but materially impossible,' he said, and at this stage, the ECSC aimed to create a common market in coal and steel and thus stifle competition among member states over natural resources. It was an idealistic creation, designed, after many centuries of conflict, to keep Europe at peace.

On 4 July 1954, food rationing came to an end in Britain, after a full fourteen years, bringing such exotic foodstuffs as bananas to the nation's tables. Change was in the air: women had had a taste of freedom in the war, just as they had had in its predecessor, and although the 1950s is often characterised as the decade of the housewife and the nuclear family, not all women were devoting themselves to house and home. A certain Margaret Hilda Thatcher, as she became when she married Denis in 1951, stood for election in 1950 and 1951, didn't contest the 1955 election because her twins, Carol and Mark, were just two and then finally entered Parliament in 1959. The idea of a female prime minister was still unthinkable at that stage, of course, but the face of Britain was beginning to change. Post-war manpower shortages had led the government to encourage far higher levels of immigration than it had ever done previously – the first wave was from Poland – and there was a significant influx from the West Indies. The first steps towards a multi-cultural Britain had begun.

Not that concerns played much part in the actual day-to-day running of most people's lives. In June 1955 the Revd Hubert Brasier and Zaidee Barnes were married, four years after Hubert's father, Tom, passed away, and on 1 October 1956, their first and only child, Theresa Mary, was born at 9 Upperton Road, a maternity hospital in Eastbourne, Sussex, where her father was the chaplain at All Saints Hospital. The family living was in the Chaplain's House – the hospital has since been converted into luxury flats. The Chapel is still used as a chapel, but whereas previously it was a place of quiet and contemplation, it is now an altogether livelier venue, hosting weddings and other events.

In the 1950s, Eastbourne itself was a lively place, a favourite among holidaymakers, with a number of theatres which attracted well-known faces including the young Bruce Forsyth, a bandstand, a pier and, not too far away, Beachy Head with its dramatic white chalk cliffs. Like many towns in post-war Britain, new housing developments sprang up: the population of the country was growing and towns and cities were getting bigger with it. Eastbourne even had its own major scandal while the infant Theresa lived there and although she was far too young to be aware of it, her parents would have known: in 1956 a local GP, Dr John Bodkin Adams, was arrested over the death of an elderly widow. The case made headlines all over the world, not least because it emerged that between 1946 and 1956 Adams had been named in 132 of his patients' wills and had also received two gifts of Rolls-Royces. There was speculation that he might have killed up to 400 people, but in the event he was found not guilty and struck off, resuming practice after just four years.

So, all in all an interesting place, but Theresa was not to be a city girl when she was growing up: she was formed by the villages of England instead. When she was three (the year Margaret Thatcher got into Parliament), the family decamped to the charming Cotswold hamlet of Church Enstone in Oxfordshire, where her father became the vicar of Enstone with Heythrop and settled into life in the local community. The Revd Brasier was a popular figure and back in the 1950s, Britain was very much a church-going nation. He and his wife and small daughter played an active role in the community, but while they were a close and loving family, duty was always at the forefront of everyone's mind. As an only child, Theresa had no siblings to escape with and no one to share the burden of being the vicar's daughter, although if truth be told she didn't seem to have considered it to be a burden – it was just the way life was.

Generosity and sharing one's good fortune were paramount, too. In 2016 *The Sun* newspaper tracked down a local who knew the family when they lived there, an eighty-seven-year-old former car-factory worker called John Watts, who had known the family decades previously. He remembered that

Theresa had had toy flatbed lorries and a red tin-plate Tri-ang Puff Puff steam engine to play with (interestingly, very much boys' toys), and when she outgrew them her parents gave them to John for his two sons. 'Her parents brought the toys down for my two boys in the 1960s after she had outgrown them,' he recalled. 'Theresa was a very pleasant and polite girl. As the daughter of the village's vicar she had a lot to live up to.'

Theresa May has said in recent years that she was aware of that, too: 'I grew up the daughter of a local vicar and the granddaughter of a regimental sergeant-major. Public service has been a part of who I am for as long as I can remember,' she commented as she was launching her bid to be prime minister. But it was a beautiful place for a child to grow up, utterly safe (no Dr Adams here), where children could roam free in a way that sometimes seems so rare today. This lovely village dates from Norman times and is dotted with buildings made from pale Cotswold stone: surrounded by fields, beech copses and glorious countryside it has a couple of pubs, a post office, shops and a primary school. Although Theresa grew up in the Swinging Sixties, there was nothing 'swinging' about a traditional hamlet like Church Enstone.

More remote then than it is now and also less exclusive, it was the place that formed her. For obvious reasons, numerous comparisons are made between Theresa May and Margaret Thatcher, not least because both were grammar-school girls from a lower middle-class background (although in terms only the British understand, Theresa was actually *middle* middle class as a vicar outranks a shopkeeper in social standing), who ended up at Oxford before going on to run the country. And while Theresa's father was a vicar, Margaret's was a Methodist lay preacher.

But in actual fact, they were very different. Maggie grew up versed in Nonconformist Methodism and learnt her politics and economics courtesy of the hard work and self-reliance embodied in her father's shop. Theresa's background was different, being that of the Church of England, the Cotswold charm and its Englishness. Theresa, as much as Margaret, understood what it was to come from a less privileged background and to work hard for success, but hers was a childhood with a slightly gentler edge. And it should not be forgotten that, unlike Margaret, she was an only child. While it would be wrong to make too much of it, it is generally accepted that only children grow up slightly faster than their sibling-laden companions, not least because they are more likely to be surrounded by adults, exposed to adult topics, expected to understand adult cares. Often they become self-contained and self-reliant and while Mrs Thatcher might have been the latter, she certainly wasn't the former. Of her as an adult, many people who have spent years working with Theresa May still don't feel as if they really know her. This dates straight back to her self-containment as a child.

But Theresa's story is littered with odd parallels not only with Britain's first female prime minister but also with that of her immediate predecessor, usually highlighting the difference between them, and this applies here too. Church Enstone is just four miles away from Dean, which is where David Cameron has his constituency and where he plays a part in the socialite Chipping Norton set, which is also about four miles away from the village. The two know the area extremely well, but while Theresa's family were surrounded by the fortunate and the wealthy, they themselves were not actually part of that world.

Church Enstone has changed since those days, too, home now to a moneyed elite and with the Renault Sport Formula One team and trendy Soho Farm nearby. But back then the family lived in the local vicarage while Hubert tended his flock at St Kenelm's Church, which dates back to Norman times, although it has been rebuilt over and again since the twelfth century. Steeped in history at home and at church and very much aware that she was the vicar's daughter, Theresa attended Heythrop Primary School, which is now closed; she herself described her first day, back in 2000, when she was one of a hundred MPs to write about their first day at school for the Pre-School Learning Alliance competition, which was published by BBC News Online. Like a lot of small children she didn't want to go to school and made a very great fuss about it indeed.

'I remember arriving at school screaming my head off because I didn't want to leave my mother,' she wrote. 'So I had to be carried into the class in the arms of the headmistress, who announced to the rest of the class: "Look what a silly little girl we've got here." Heythrop Primary was a very small school with only 27 children in the whole school, and when I left, there were only 11 children. Mrs Williams, the headmistress, was the only teacher. I also remember that when the sun shone we used to take our desks outside, and sometimes when the ice cream van came, we all got an ice cream if we had been very good.'

Not the rebel, then, and she never became one, either. As an adult it has accurately been remarked that Theresa May has no wild side and that was also the case back then. At home, her mother taught her how to make scones, and cooking became a lasting passion, with the adult Theresa owning more than a hundred cookbooks. Her father, Hubert, meanwhile, passed his love of cricket on to his daughter and together the two of them would listen to it on the radio, with Theresa idolising not the likes of the Rolling Stones or the Beatles, but the cricketer Geoff Boycott. As an adult she was to campaign (unsuccessfully) for Boycott to be awarded a knighthood: 'I have been a Geoff Boycott fan all my life,' she once told the *Daily Telegraph*. 'It was just that he kind of solidly got on with what he was doing.'

The 1960s were now well under way and the face of Britain continued to change. In the 1950s, mass immigration had led to some racial tensions, which were still ongoing and now attempts had begun to control the flow of people coming into the country. The problem, somewhat ironically in view of what was to lead directly to Mrs May's taking up residence at Number 10, was that there had been no controls on anyone coming in from the Empire and later the Commonwealth – the organisation composed of fifty-three member states that had once been part of the Empire. But such numbers were coming in that the various governments of the day found themselves under increasing pressure to do something about it, with the result that in the course of one decade, three separate pieces of legislation were passed to make it more difficult for immigrants to come in.

And while it is only decades later that the full extent of changes in society became apparent as the sixties trundled along, the old-style establishment in Britain was falling and a considerably less hidebound version was taking its place. The satire boom of the 1960s had done what had never been done before: it had openly mocked the political class and in particular the Prime Minister, Harold Macmillan. London was swinging (or as someone more accurately put it, about 200 people in London were swinging, while everyone else was carrying on as normal) and class barriers were beginning to fall. In the 1960s, a whole host of working-class actors started to emerge, including the likes of Michael Caine, Roger Moore (whose father was a south London policeman) and Terence Stamp. In other words, to be working class not only didn't hold you back, it was positively fashionable as exemplified by the likes of the photographer David Bailey and the artist David Hockney. There were hippies, short skirts, Flower Power and the Summer of Love. Other exciting innovations were going on too. By the time Theresa May entered her teens, there had been a man on the moon. None of this might have impinged on her little village but the world outside was changing.

Even so, there were standards to be maintained at home. Theresa was very much aware of the fact that she was the vicar's daughter and she was determined not to let her parents down. She behaved properly, responsibly, was not at all flashy and didn't show off. In fact, teenage rebellion was never an issue. 'You don't think about it at the time, but there are certain responsibilities that come with being the vicar's daughter,' she said in an interview with the *Daily Telegraph* in 2012. 'You're supposed to behave in a particular way. I shouldn't say it, but I probably was Goody Two Shoes.' The entire family was conscious of their duties to the village in which they lived and indeed to wider society: current affairs would be discussed over the dinner table, creating, 'a natural environment to seek a political future,' as Theresa herself once remarked.

Theresa was a studious girl, as she herself admits, and by her teens was slightly self-conscious about how tall she had become, with contemporaries remembering her hunching her shoulders slightly to distract from her height. Somewhat surprisingly for the daughter of a C of E vicar, she then went on to study at St Juliana's Convent School for Girls, a Catholic School in Begbroke (which closed in 1984), before at the age of thirteen winning a scholarship to Holton Park Girls'

Grammar School in Wheatley, Oxon, which was based in the manor house and grounds of the Holton Park estate.

It was a place redolent of history: Oliver Cromwell had used it as his base during the Civil War and it was here that his daughter Bridget married Henry Ireton in 1646. Later, it was owned by some of England's most notable families, namely the Biscoes, Briggses and Balfours. During World War II it housed the 97th American Field Hospital and in 1948 the Balfours sold it to Oxfordshire County Council, which said it should house a school.

East Oxfordshire Girls' Grammar School, formerly in Thame, moved into the new place and under the headships of Miss Davies and Mrs Mills the school became very successful academically and started sending many girls to university before that became the norm. So much of Theresa May's life as a politician can be traced back to those early years: it is notable that when she came to form her first Cabinet, not only was there a very healthy representation of former grammar-school pupils, but one of the first potential new non-Brexit-related policies to float out from the inner sanctum was the reinstatement of grammar schools.

Theresa had personal experience of their wanton destruction under a Labour Party that did not understand they had given intelligent students from less privileged backgrounds a chance to succeed: in 1971, when she was fifteen, the school was abolished and became part of Wheatley Park Comprehensive School. It was part of the great destruction of an educational system that had worked wonders for generations: anyone who passed the 11-plus would be granted a place at a grammar school regardless of their financial background; and it was one of the many reasons why social class became far more fluid in twentieth-century Britain because it gave pupils from poorer backgrounds access to a first-class educational system. But the Labour Party had taken against it on the grounds that it was elitist and condemned those who didn't pass the 11-plus to a second-rate life. From the mid-1960s Labour embarked on a strategy to destroy the system completely, with the socialist Anthony Crosland, a disastrous Education Secretary from 1965 to 1967, informing his wife Susan, 'If it's the last thing I do, I'm going to destroy every fucking grammar school in England. And in Wales and Northern Ireland.'

Theresa May was on the ground, so to speak, when this plan was put into action and was an eyewitness to quite what a disaster this policy turned out to be. However, she had already benefited from her time at the school and very early on had made up her mind what she wanted to do. Around the age of twelve she decided on a career in politics and notified her parents; both were encouraging. However, Hubert, as the local vicar, was concerned that his daughter might compromise his position and so asked her to be discreet. Theresa largely stood by this request but got in touch with her local Conservative Association and would quietly spend afternoons there stuffing envelopes and – who knows? – perhaps dreaming of a time when she might enter Number 10. Much of the remainder of her spare time was devoted to reading and the only concession as the 1970s approached was fashion, with an eye for clothes that even back then would stand out: 'Flared trousers and a yellow blouse that had huge voluminous sleeves,' she later told BBC Radio 4 *Desert Island Discs*, and it is perhaps no surprise that the 1970s should be known as the decade that style forgot. (Although in fairness to Theresa, everyone was dressed like that!)

That outing, on *Desert Island Discs* in 2014, which featured two hymns, was the first glimpse the wider public got into the childhood of a woman who had by that time already become a political heavyweight. People were becoming increasingly curious about the then Home Secretary, then as now not prone to revealing a good deal about herself, although she did oblige with some insights into her past life. Not that much of it would have been a surprise. Asked by presenter Kirsty Young if she was a conscientious student, Theresa replied: 'I'm afraid so, yes. I enjoyed reading, I did my homework, I was that sort of schoolgirl.' As for her father's profession, she not only accepted it but was a practising Christian herself right from the start: 'At no stage did I take issue with the Church . . . I didn't feel the need to kick the traces.'

She went on to talk about how religion had dominated all their lives. 'Obviously everything did very much revolve around the Church,' she explained. 'Early memories of a father who couldn't always be there when you wanted him to be, but he was around quite a lot of the time and other times when parents weren't normally. I have one memory, for example, of being in the kitchen and looking up the path to the back door, where a whole group, a family, that had come to complain about an issue in the church and that's it, just knock on the door and expect to see the vicar.' But church was 'never imposed' on her, she emphasised, and indeed she has remained a church-goer all her life.

Her school, like most good, academic institutions at the time, had a debating society, and while this was an area in which one day Theresa would excel, she didn't get off to a good start: 'I went up to the front and I picked a piece of paper [from the hat] and I turned round and I couldn't think of a single thing to say, so my career in debating started with silence,' she told Kirsty Young, although that didn't put her off when she went up to Oxford, where her real talent as a debater began to emerge.

In 2016, just a few days before Theresa May became Prime Minister, a book by Marilyn Yurdan was published entitled *School Songs and Gymslips*, which was about Holton Park Grammar School in the 1960s and 70s. Theresa wrote the introduction and it summed up her teenage years as little else she has said has done:

> Despite covering a period only just over fifty years ago, it seems like a different world. This book brings back so many memories – from sherbet fountains to

Corona, from Tommy Steele to *Z Cars*, from stodgy puddings to Vesta curries; and that's not to mention the education. How different from today's world of the internet, yet children now will have their favourite teachers and the not so favourite, will still try to find ways out of doing homework and will still make lifelong friendships at school.

Theresa was also obeying her father's stricture not to make her interest in politics too public, but that didn't stop her from standing in Holton Park's mock general election in 1974 when she was doing her A-levels. Already showing signs of quite unusual academic ability, she had been moved up a year and stood as a Tory against her fellow student Rosalind Hicks-Greene (as she became after her marriage), who stood as a Liberal. Rosalind won and somewhat ironically was pictured on Friday, 1 March 1974 on the front page of the *Oxford Times* with the headline: 'The new Prime Minister!' Beside her, Theresa is pictured, tall, slightly hunch-shouldered, shy but smiling in defeat. Was it then that steel entered her soul? It takes a good deal of tenacity to get into politics and even more so to succeed at the very top level, and this early experience may well have given her an insight into what it would be like in later life. Clearly it was not just top public schools like Eton that prepared pupils to run the country, the humbler grammar schools did a pretty good job of it as well.

'There was a general election in the country and it was the

school's tradition to hold a mock one at the same time,' Mrs Hicks-Greene told the *Daily Mail* in 2016 when a further wave of interest in Theresa May's early years prompted journalists to start digging around for the people she knew when she was young. 'It's hard to say why I won. I was head girl at school and that was something you were voted into, it was a popularity contest. We both gave a speech about what we thought were the policies of our respective parties, and in those days Liberal policies were much more appealing to a young audience than Conservative policies.'

Another element that worked against Theresa was that she 'wasn't very charismatic at school. She was very serious and quite reserved and that probably didn't go in her favour,' said Hicks-Greene. But while she didn't think that Mrs May would want such a high-profile role as prime minister, 'She gives everything a lot of research and won't arrive at ideas without consideration, but once she is on a course she follows it through. I thought she would be a university lecturer or something. She was very quiet and studious but when she needed to make her views felt, she certainly could do so.'

Oddly enough when Margaret Thatcher first started trying to get into politics, she too didn't exhibit the charisma that was so obvious later on and by all accounts wasn't very good in her early attempts at public speaking, although she soon learned.

As did Theresa May. Already interested in politics, she was fairly sure that that was where her future lay, but unlike so many of her peers, she was to work in the 'real world' before finally getting a seat. That, too, was in the future, however, because university was now on the cards. Theresa had attended a highly academic school and gained the kind of education the fortunate did before the grammar schools were destroyed, and now she was to go on to attend one of the best universities in the world. Academic and well read, Theresa's time at Oxford would not just provide her with an education, but give further insight into the practice of politics and expose her to a wider world than the one she was brought up in. While she was there, for the first time in its history a woman was elected as the Leader of the Conservative Party, something that cannot have failed to make a huge impression on the young student. And if that were not enough, she'd be meeting her future husband, too.

4

DREAMING SPIRES

Oxford University, the oldest seat of learning in the UK and the second oldest in the world. Oxford University, the city of dreaming spires (as opposed to Cambridge, the university of perspiring dreams!), bastion of elitism and alma mater to many a prime minister, including Margaret Thatcher and David Cameron, and now Theresa Brasier, too. Oxford University, that fiercely competitive cradle of academia, training ground for aspiring politicians and much else, and a beautiful and ancient city to boot, establishing its students with an address book that would benefit them for the rest of their lives, a letter of introduction to the portals of the great and good, a source of kudos recognised all over the world.

Just getting in was an achievement and the young Theresa was to do a lot more than that, making a success of her time there and building up contacts who to this day remain friends and colleagues. It was quite a leap from being a domestic: history does not record what Theresa's two grandmothers made of their granddaughter's passport to privilege, but chances are both were delighted. It was already obvious that Theresa was academic and ambitious and now she was attending one of the two best universities in the UK, on track for a hugely successful career.

Oxford University is different from most British universities, operating a college system that only a handful of others share. It dates back to 1096 and like Cambridge is divided into a series of self-governing colleges, currently thirty-eight, and students apply not to the university, but to the college, which is where they will live for some or all of their time at Oxford and where their studies will be based. Every college has a director of studies in every discipline it teaches, alongside further numbers of dons, fellows, professors and lecturers; the student will attend tutorials both inside the college and to a lesser extent outside. The academic departments themselves are university wide, with each college having tutors and professors that are part of those departments.

Like Cambridge, there is no campus as such: colleges and the many communal buildings such as the Radcliffe Camera, the Sheldonian Theatre, the Examination Rooms and more are scattered throughout the city: individually and as a whole, Oxford, the university and the city, is so beautiful that it attracts large numbers of tourists, especially during the spring term. It is larger than Cambridge, which is essentially a university with a city tacked on the edges: Oxford is a city in itself, with all the amenities most cities provide and it is also only an hour away on the train to London. It was a stepping stone of sorts from her life as a child to that of an adult: not too far from where Theresa had been brought up, it was also going to be her gateway into the wider world.

Just as Oxford is not set up the way most universities are, so the rites and traditions hark back to an earlier and more civilised world. Students still wear formal dress for matriculation and exams and most colleges hold balls at the end of the academic year. Colleges also have 'formal halls', which again require formal dress and at which a Latin grace is said, and the number of times they are held in the week of the month differs with the college. Otherwise students would eat at the college buttery or make their own arrangements (Theresa, a very keen cook, would have been more than capable there.)

The social life of Oxford is extremely active and to a certain extent very competitive, with students rivalling each other to see how many invitations to garden parties, sherry parties and much else that they can accrue and placing the 'stiffies' – hard cards embossed with the time and the place – on their mantelpieces for all to see. Any number of clubs and societies exist to cater to student interests and indeed to prepare them for later life, most notably, in Theresa's case, the Union Society (not to be confused with the Student Union), of which more below.

As with everywhere and everything else, women were only allowed into the party late and it was not until 1875 – just a century before Theresa's arrival – that Oxford University passed a statute allowing delegates to create exams for women on something approximating an undergraduate level. There were further battles to fight: it was not until 1920 that they were given the right to take degrees (in Cambridge, it was 1948). Shortly after that earlier statute the women's colleges began to appear: Lady Margaret Hall in 1878, Somerville in 1879, St Hugh's in 1886, St Hilda's in 1893 and St Anne's College in 1952. All accepted only women until relatively recently (St Hilda's being the last to open its doors to men in 2008), when the other Oxford colleges finally began to turn co-ed.

Theresa was offered a place at St Hugh's, an attractive college set in large gardens and founded by William Wordsworth's niece Elizabeth Wordsworth, using money left to her by her father, the Bishop of Lincoln. Naturally this was appropriate for the daughter of a man of the cloth and the name of the college came from an earlier Bishop of Lincoln, Hugh of Avalon, with Oxford forming part of his diocese. Theresa May is not the only notable female politician to have passed through its doors: others include Barbara Castle, Nicky Morgan and the Burmese politician and Nobel Prize winner Aung San Suu Kyi. But despite the presence of the women's colleges, Oxford was still a male-dominated establishment back then (more good training for the House of Commons) and there was none of the exhibitionist female behaviour you sometimes see today: 'We weren't girly,' a contemporary recalled. 'If you got into Oxford as a woman back then, you had a certain inner strength.' And they needed it – there was no shortage of male dons or male students only too happy to put the women down.

Many future politicians at Oxford choose to study history or politics, philosophy and economics (PPE), but Theresa, slightly more surprisingly perhaps, opted for geography. It is not seen as one of the more academic subjects at Oxford, although as her opponents were to learn later to their cost, to underestimate her intellect is to make a bad mistake. But her intake of geography students turned out to be an extraordinary one: quite a few of Theresa's peers at St Hugh's went on to carve out very high-achieving lives for themselves, of which more below.

Most first years live in the main body of the building. Theresa matriculated in 1974 – as with Cambridge, Oxford graduates are always classed by the year they enter the institution, not the year they leave, in part to reflect the fact that different degrees take different lengths of time – and a photograph of her year shows her on the first row, looking demure in the traditional dress of black skirt, with shirt, black gown and black tights (no kitten heels here). Just seventeen at the time, she was one of nine students at the college studying geography: one of them was Alicia Collinson, then and now a friend of Theresa's, who went on to become a very successful family law barrister married to another politico and Oxford contemporary (promoted when Mrs May became PM), Damian Green.

Another is Louise Rowe, now Lady Patten, who carved out a spectacular career in the City and married John, now Lord, Patten, an erstwhile Home Office minister under Margaret Thatcher and Secretary of State for Education under John Major, who also studied geography at Oxford and, a few years older than Louise, taught political geography at the university both to Theresa and his future wife. He would have been a strong influence on Theresa as a further classmate recalls.

For another who studied geography in that year was Denise Patterson, née Palmer, who became a successful literary agent: 'John Patten was one of our tutors,' she told the *Daily Telegraph* in July 2016. 'He taught us political geography. He almost certainly had an influence on Theresa. Theresa was always interested in politics in a quiet, serious way. She wasn't a flamboyant character but she had this burning ambition.' Denise herself went on to marry Jack Patterson, aka the novelist Jack Higgins, author of *The Eagle Has Landed*.

There must have been something in the water that year (although it is hardly unknown for Oxford graduates to do spectacularly well in life) for yet another high achiever who matriculated in 1974 was Emma Hood, née Saunders. Theresa was 'always very focused on going into politics,' she told the *Daily Telegraph*. 'I remember her saying, "One day I will lead the [Conservative] Party." Theresa had this steely determination to make the grade at a very senior level in politics.' Lady Hood herself went on to marry Sir John Hood, a former vice-chancellor of the university.

David Cameron, who attended Oxford University a decade later, famously became a member of the Bullingdon Club (as did Boris Johnson), that outpost of gilded youth born to privilege and to sit above the salt. Theresa's time at Oxford contained nothing whatsoever along those lines: she was not a member of any similar society and there are no tales at all of riotous behaviour or unruly conduct involving farm animals. The political backdrop for the two premiers at their time at university was very different, too. Mr Cameron attended Oxford University at the height of Thatcherism; Theresa, on the other hand, was experiencing all the chaos that led up to it. In the mid-1970s Britain was commonly perceived to be the 'sick man of Europe', with unions attempting to dominate politics, strikes, the three-day week, chaos and finally the country's humiliating financial bailout by the International Monetary Fund (IMF) in 1976. There were also power cuts, which meant that students had to study by candlelight.

Theresa settled fast into university life. Unsurprisingly she worked hard, just as she had at school: 'very determined and diligent,' recalled one contemporary whom *The Observer* tracked down in 2014. 'You know, she did what it said on the tin. She would do the work while I got drunk.' Then as now, Theresa didn't do hanging out at the bar with her contemporaries, she just got on with the job in hand.

But the interest in politics that she had had from an early

age grew, and while at twelve she had merely set her sights on becoming an MP, now she decided to aim a little higher, with a shot at being PM. Not that anyone would have taken her seriously, at that stage, because even though Margaret Thatcher was on the verge of becoming the Leader of the Conservative Party, there were very many who thought she would never actually win an election simply because she was the wrong sex. But that didn't seem to worry Theresa. 'My memory's hazy, but it was the first term at Oxford in 1974,' said her friend Alicia Collinson. 'We were at breakfast and she said something about wanting to be Prime Minister.' An interesting comparison is with Michael Heseltine, who was also at Oxford when he confessed to the same ambition, famously jotting down the years he believed the various glittering prizes would come tumbling into his lap on the back of an envelope. In the event, of course, he never achieved it. The more modest (and less hubristic) Theresa May did.

One of her contemporaries at Oxford was Pat Frankland, who also enrolled in 1974 and has remained a close chum. She too remembered Theresa voicing her ambitions when most people would have thought such a thing impossible. 'She wanted to be the first woman prime minister back in our Oxford days and she was very irritated when Maggie Thatcher beat her to it,' Pat, now a retired economics and business teacher, recalled shortly after Theresa gained the keys to Number 10, speaking to *The Guardian*. 'It was just – "I wanted to be first and she got there first". I met her on our first or second day of college, when she was seventeen and I was eighteen. I was aware of that ambition from the very early days. She used to drag me along to political lectures.'

Another friend, speaking when Theresa was Home Secretary, said that Theresa admired Margaret Thatcher, but that, 'I think that admiration was for what Thatcher was doing as a woman rather than her politics. I knew Theresa was interested in politics but there were no intimations back then that she would end up where she has. Did I think it was obvious she was going to become Home Secretary? No.'

Theresa became a member of the Oxford Union Society, always known as the Oxford Union, a debating society founded in 1823 and the de facto ground of many a future politician, who learned not only how to speak fluently and think on their feet, but also gained a view into the dark arts of political assassinations, something that was widely commented on when Michael Gove stabbed Boris Johnson in the back (both were Presidents of the Union). Standing in its own freestanding debating chamber, which was designed by Alfred Waterhouse and opened in 1879, it contains a bar, a dining room, where the very many famous guest speakers are entertained, a library, a snooker room and much more. In the debating chamber itself the set-up is slightly reminiscent of the House of Commons, presided over by the President and assorted others. It cannot be overemphasised how influential the Oxford Union is, not only in training up one generation of politicians after another, but in one case, at least, possibly influencing historical events.

In 1933, in the most controversial episode in its history, the Union debated the motion, 'that this House will in no circumstances fight for its King and Country', which it carried by 275 votes to 153. The uproar it provoked extended far beyond the dreaming spires: the 'sensation created when this resolution was passed was tremendous,' wrote the historian R. B. McCallum. 'It received world-wide publicity. Throughout England people, especially elderly people, were thoroughly shocked. Englishmen who were in India at the time have told me of the dismay they felt when they heard of it. "What is wrong with the younger generation?" was the general query.'

The press, including the *Daily Telegraph* and the *Manchester Guardian*, picked up on the story, while the *Daily Express* reflected the widespread view of the time: 'There is no question but that the woozy-minded Communists, the practical jokers, and the sexual indeterminates of Oxford have scored a great success in the publicity that has followed this victory. Even the plea of immaturity, or the irresistible passion of the undergraduate for posing, cannot excuse such a contemptible and indecent action as the passing of that resolution,' it opined.

Winston Churchill went further still, warning how this would be taken overseas: 'My mind turns across the narrow waters of Channel and the North Sea, where great nations stand determined to defend their national glories or national existence with their lives,' he said in a speech to the Anti-Socialist and Anti-Communist Union. 'I think of Germany, with its splendid clear-eyed youths marching forward on all the roads of the Reich singing their ancient songs, demanding to be conscripted into an army; eagerly seeking the most terrible weapons of war; burning to suffer and die for their fatherland. I think of Italy, with her ardent Fascisti, her renowned Chief, and stern sense of national duty. I think of France, anxious, peace-loving, pacifist to the core, but armed to the teeth and determined to survive as a great nation in the world. One can almost feel the curl of contempt upon the lips of the manhood of all these people when they read this message sent out by Oxford University in the name of young England.' He was right to be concerned – many believe that the Nazi Party, then in the ascendancy in Germany, took note of the seeming refusal of the youth of England to fight for their country and it had a direct influence on German expansionism and ultimately war. The Japanese were said to have noted the result, too.

No such controversy erupted when Theresa May was there. The Union is run by a standing committee elected by the students, with a president, president elect, junior librarian, junior treasurer, librarian-elect, treasurer-elect and secretary as well as a raft of other roles and these roles are both coveted and extremely viciously fought for. Past presidents include such luminaries as William Gladstone, Edward Heath, Tony Benn, Michael Heseltine and William Hague, to name but a few. The oddity in Theresa's case, however, was that although she became a returning officer, she didn't actually seek elected office in the Union itself, another reason why most people did not realise they had a rising star in their midst. The big names of the day when Theresa May was at Oxford were David Willetts, Damian Green, Alan Duncan and Dominic Grieve, alongside her future husband Philip May, who also became president, while Benazir Bhutto, glamorous, well connected, from one of Pakistan's leading families and ultimately destined for a tragic end, outshone the lot of them.

Theresa didn't seem to be in the same league, not least because of the lack of showiness that was to serve her so well in later life. 'She was always more ambitious than any of us noticed,' commented one university friend. 'The truth is that in student elections you're trying to impress 300 people who are all friends, and she didn't have that kind of personality.' Perhaps she was repelled by the vicious infighting, perhaps, always supremely pragmatic, she reasoned there was no need to make any enemies who would be carried on into later life (the highest level of politics is riddled with people who cordially loathe each other because of the way they all behaved some forty years previously). In a strange way her reluctance to stand foreshadows her vanishing act in the EU referendum many years later: why put yourself on the line when you don't have to? Why not wait until the time is right to make a move?

'She was very, very well liked,' a friend told *The Observer* years later, in July 2014. 'I think part of the reason she never stood for election at the Union was that she wasn't a machinating politician. She wasn't somebody who would curry the support of different sides. She wasn't factional.' That may have been so, but it did lead observers to speculate in recent years quite what it must have been like for those contemporaries, who so effortlessly outshone her, to have to watch Theresa May snatch the highest prizes, with one insider confiding, 'I always wondered how it must have felt that Damian has been playing second fiddle to Theresa.' However it felt, the Tories are a pragmatic crew, though, as exemplified by the speed and efficiency with which they got Theresa into Number 10 when the moment came, and none of her Oxford contemporaries have spoken publicly, at least, about how it felt to be so overshadowed in the fullness of time.

However, Theresa did debate at the Union, learning to speak confidently and fluently, and she was also very political herself. Indeed many students were. 'It was a generation that was very much turned against that left-wing nature of the Sixties,' said Damian Green in later years. 'We were the next generation up that became Thatcher's children. In that period when the Labour government was just running into the ground, the Conservative Association was very strong.' And Theresa proved herself able to speak with passion and conviction: in a contemporary report on a debate about abortion, she was described as 'the statuesque Miss Brasier, burning with emotion in her red dress'. (Clothes clearly played a part back then, too.)

Theresa, like so many other senior Tories, was a member of the Oxford University Conservative Association (OUCA), another breeding ground for future politicians, which also had elections and was frequently dominated by the same people who spoke in the Union. The turbulent political background at the time caused it to split sharply between left and right (much as the parliamentary party was doing) but Theresa again, and not for the last time, managed to find a path which kept her somehow in the middle. Unusually, she wasn't associated with either side. 'She was coming at it more as a kind of moral thing than from a sort of curiosity,' a contemporary told *The Guardian* in February 2015.

Her friend Alicia Collinson described Mrs May as 'fun' at Oxford, and she did and does have a lighter side than she is normally credited with, becoming a member of the Edmund Burke Society, a tongue-in-cheek alternative to the Oxford Union, with debates of a far more satirical nature. Michael Crick and Damian Green were also members. Unlike the Union, Theresa ran for office. The society held debates on Sunday nights at the Morris room of the Union, where they would drink copious amounts of port out of tiny glasses ('they' probably not including Theresa). In the third term of her last year she became president, coming up with a series of satirical topics including, 'This House thanks Heaven for little girls' and 'Life's too short for chess', clearly enjoying herself hugely as she waved a meat tenderiser at her fellow students in place of a gavel.

She had some unlikely hinterlands, too. One friend recalled, 'Theresa and I used to love watching *The Goodies*' – the mildly anarchic BBC comedy television show that ran throughout the 1970s and early 80s, starring Bill Oddie, Tim Brooke-Taylor and Graeme Garden. (All three participants are livid that the BBC refuses to repeat it. The grounds for the decision are not clear but it may well have been because the show was so irredeemably naff.) Alongside the politics there was religion, a constant throughout Theresa's life. She attended church every Sunday but then, as now, kept it as a private part of her life.

Two years after matriculating, Theresa met Philip May, her first and only serious boyfriend and the man she would go on to wed. 'Theresa went out with other people,' said Alicia Collinson. 'But none of them were quite what she wanted. None of them were special. Then in our final year, Philip came along. There was Philip and nobody else.' They were introduced to each other at a Conservative Association dance by Benazir Bhutto in 1976: 'He was good-looking and there was an immediate attraction,' said Theresa, in an extremely rare insight into her personal life. 'We danced, though I can't remember the music.'

Philip was born in Norfolk in 1957, making him a year younger than his wife-to-be (although academically he was two years behind), to John, a sales rep for a shoe wholesaler – something that caused a few wry smiles in later years given Theresa's love of footwear – and Joy, a part-time

French language teacher at an all-girls' school. Like Theresa, Philip was a grammar school student: the family moved to Merseyside when he was still very young and he was a student at Calday Grange Grammar School. They shared a love of cricket, with Theresa harbouring a soft spot for West Indian fast bowler Tony Gray back then.

Philip studied history at Lincoln College and became president of the Union Society, taking over from the future Tory MP Alan Duncan and succeeded by the future journalist Michael Crick. Ironically, it was always assumed that he would be the one to go on to enjoy the big political career and in later years there were rumours that they had the same arrangement as Tony and Cherie Blair – whichever one found a seat first would get to have the political career. But right from the start, he brought out Theresa's more human side, making her laugh and relax in his company. With Philip, she would let down her guard. 'Phil was a lot of fun,' a contemporary of the couple told *The Observer*. 'He had loads of levity – but she did too. It's a myth she wasn't jolly because she was. She was good fun. She would come up with witticisms and quips. She would make jokes – lots of them cricketing jokes, to be fair.'

Theresa graduated in 1977 with a second-class degree in geography. She moved to London, but her relationship with her boyfriend went from strength to strength. Philip, meanwhile, became president of the Union during the course of which he met former US President Richard Nixon, and also invited his girlfriend back in 1979 to oppose the motion

'That sex is good . . . but success is better'. Theresa's exact speech and indeed the outcome of the debate have been lost in the mists of time but it did at least show that the two of them shared a sense of humour, possibly one of the most important foundations for a solid marriage. Theirs had indeed become a very strong relationship, one that was to provide Theresa with much-needed comfort and support in the often troubled and challenging years ahead.

5

TRIUMPH – AND TRAGEDY

Theresa Brasier graduated from Oxford in 1977, her university years behind her (academically, at least – with a boyfriend still in situ, she still went back quite a bit). But the time had come to turn her thoughts to the world of work. A charge that is often levelled against modern politicians is that they have no experience outside the political sphere, leaving the rarefied atmosphere of university, usually Oxford or Cambridge, to work at a think tank, as a special adviser to an MP, or any number of realms far away from most people's experience of life.

That is not the case with Theresa Brasier, who in fact carved out a career in the City, something that was surprisingly overlooked during the Conservative leadership race of 2016, when her rival Andrea Leadsom's financial credentials were brandished as proof of fitness to run the economy. But Theresa's working life before becoming an MP, which lasted for twenty years, was also spent in the City. She was there during a time of stratospheric change, when the old-school merchant banks and stockbrokers of yesteryear were bought up by global institutions, when insider trading was made illegal, a move that didn't happen until 1980, and when the Big Bang took place in 1986.

A cornerstone of Margaret Thatcher's policies, the Big Bang opened up the markets, put an end to the old boy network which was strongly prevalent up to then, and comprehensively established the City of London as the world's foremost financial centre, boosted by its geographical position as being halfway between the United States and the Far East and the fact that the universal language of English is spoken there. The status of the City of London has frequently been a point of contention within the EU itself and it is often forgotten that Theresa had a ringside seat, watching it transform into a global financial force.

After leaving Oxford, Theresa went to work for the Bank of England, where she would stay for the next six years. Nestling on Threadneedle Street in the heart of the City, the world's second oldest central bank, which was established in 1694, is housed in grand premises opposite the Royal Exchange. Very little information exists about this time in Theresa's life, but she would almost certainly have gone into a standard job in one of the divisions such as the international division and is unlikely to have had anything to do with markets or policy.

The City itself was virtually unrecognisable to modern eyes: this was an era when the men really did still wear bowler hats and carry furled umbrellas, while London itself was nothing like the glittering metropolis it is today. This was still the dying days of the Callaghan government, the Lib-Lab pact and the Winter of Discontent, which sealed the pact's fate, the attempt by the unions to dominate the course of government. Margaret Thatcher was Tory Party Leader and a revolution was in the making, but the end of the 1970s showed Britain to be tired, depressed and nowhere near recovery from being the sick man of Europe. And as for the food . . . London was certainly not the gastronomic paradise it was to become.

But what did Theresa care? She was young, freshly arrived in the capital and there was all to play for. Her career proper had begun – although it wouldn't be long before she returned to her first interest, politics, and started making waves there, too. It was also very obvious now that she had met the man she was going to marry, which would have the effect of providing her with emotional stability both in her career and during a highly turbulent period in her early twenties. To begin with, at least, Philip was still at Oxford, although as he neared the end of his time there, it became increasingly clear to everyone that this was the relationship each had been looking for and that they would wed.

They had been together for three years by now, and showed no sign of parting, but even so the student newspaper,

Cherwell, ran a mischievous gossip piece about the couple: 'I gather the same fate [rejection] awaits Philip if he hesitates any longer in announcing his intention to make an honest woman of the Vicar's daughter,' it somewhat snidely claimed. The implication was that Theresa had issued Philip with an ultimatum, which seems very out of character, not to mention unnecessary. It was yet another example, though, of Oxford preparing them both for the wider world. Just as student politicians began to learn their trade beneath the dreaming spires, so too the journalists of tomorrow did exactly the same and *Cherwell* was one of the places they started. Theresa (and very occasionally Philip) would have to put up with an awful lot of comment from the media later in life, and so that early experience would have prepared her for what was to come.

At any rate, by Philip's last summer term, during which he was president of the Oxford Union, they became engaged and were married in September 1980 at the Church of St Mary the Virgin, where Theresa's father was vicar. A wedding photo shows the pair looking deliriously happy, with Theresa's mother, Zaidee, who was by then suffering from multiple sclerosis, in a wheelchair beside them. This was to be the start of a long, happy and very stable union, but there was trauma in store too.

It could have been reasonably expected that Theresa and Philip would have had a happy few years together before starting a family, but nothing went as might have been planned and for all the enduring closeness of the relationship, there was a tragic start to their married life. Just a year after they wed, the Revd Brasier was driving in his Morris Marina to a nearby church in Forest Hill, where he was due to conduct a service. He was trying to cross the busy A40 when he was in a collision with a Range Rover, with fatal results.

According to the subsequent inquest, he 'edged forward from the central reservation into the path of a Range Rover'. The driver of the other car, containing three passengers, attempted to stop in time but it was too late: the cars crashed at speed and a few hours later Theresa's father died of head and spine injuries. He was sixty-four. Theresa, an only child who was very close to her father, was devastated. Losing a parent is extremely hard whatever the circumstances, but to have a father in good health snatched away so abruptly and at such a relatively young age seemed undeniably cruel, especially so soon after she had married. And she had no siblings to share the pain with – only Philip, who fairly soon was going to constitute the only close family she had.

It was a tragedy for all concerned, with Theresa losing her father, Zaidee, who was very ill herself, being left a widow, and of course the trauma experienced by those in the other car. The driver of the Range Rover was chartered surveyor Desmond Hampton – who was in no way at fault – and he was driving home to west London with his wife Kitty and their two daughters, Emma and Vanessa. Emma Groslin as she now is, a parish councillor in Hampshire and married with children, was actually unaware of the fact that the person in the other car was the Revd Brasier until Theresa May became Prime Minister and *The Sun* newspaper tracked her down. She was clearly jolted by the news. 'I knew it was a local vicar and he had been on his way to give his last service of the day,' she said in an interview in July 2016. 'I had no idea he was Theresa May's father until now. It's shocking – it was an awful event. We were on our way from Gloucestershire on a dual carriageway back to London after visiting our grandparents. I was asleep in the back of the car with my younger sister and the next thing I knew, I woke up and it had happened.'

Her father Desmond, who died in 2014, told the inquest, 'I noticed the Marina stationary in the central reservation and it appeared to stay there for quite a bit of time. It appeared to move slowly and then hesitate. I began braking and tried to get in the left-hand lane.' The Oxfordshire coroner Nicholas Gardiner, recording a verdict of accidental death, noted the crossing had both slow local traffic and fast, long-distance traffic: 'That's never a good thing as far as road safety is concerned,' he said.

Two families were shattered by the turn of events; it was a dark period in the young Theresa's life. And as if that were not bad enough, Zaidee died just one year after that, at the age of fifty-four. Because of the multiple sclerosis this was not quite so unexpected, but to lose two parents so close together was a heavy blow. Theresa was effectively an orphan in her early twenties and, again, there were no siblings with whom to share the pain, or indeed, share old memories of childhood. Were it not for Philip, she would have been very alone. Theresa, never one to wear her heart on her sleeve, has not spoken at length about this double tragedy, but in the space of just a year she had gone from newly married daughter to the mourner of two parents. The fact that she could turn to her husband in her hour of need was not just a sign of the fact that she had chosen well but it was also a positive augur for the trials that lay ahead in her political life.

But Philip provided the emotional support she needed as Theresa told presenter Kirsty Young on BBC Radio 4's *Desert Island Discs*: 'Crucially I had huge support in my husband and that was very important for me,' she said. 'I mean, he was a real rock for me. He has been all the time we've been married, but particularly then of course being faced with the loss of both parents within a relatively short space of time.' That was understating the case. Although Philip remained popular and convivial, over time the two of them were to form what would sometimes seem an impregnable unit, a fortress against the outside world that both – and particularly Theresa – could shelter behind when the slings and arrows of outrageous fortune simply became too much to bear. A union that is hit by early tragedy can in some cases be strengthened by it and that is what happened here.

Their friends knew it, too. They had kept in touch with a lot of the Oxford crowd, who were now also taking their first steps towards forging their careers, and it was obvious to everyone that Philip provided the emotional support that

Theresa needed in her darkest hour. People spoke of his devotion and as the decade progressed and it slowly became apparent that it was going to be Theresa, not Philip, who was destined for a glittering political career, he never showed the slightest sign of resentment or jealousy – quite the opposite. Of those terrible events, Theresa's friend Alicia Collinson later told the *Sunday Telegraph*, 'It was dreadful. Theresa had Philip and Philip saw her through that. He was and remains her rock.'

She would need him in later years, too, when she faced not tragedy, but the challenges of politics in opposition – and finally on the front line.

Once he had graduated, a couple of years after Theresa, and moved down to London, Philip too started to carve out a career for himself. Like his wife, he went into finance: he became a graduate trainee analyst at de Zoete & Bevan, a traditional stockbroker, which after he left would end up subsumed into Barclays de Zoete Wedd, or BZW – Barclays created its investment banking arm by acquiring de Zoete and the jobber Wedd Durlacher in response to the Big Bang. While there, Philip went into equity fund management, a position he held from 1979 to 1983, and was remembered by colleagues as being 'extremely bright, quite quiet and very diligent'. In 1983 he moved to Prudential Portfolio Managers, where he stayed until 2000. This was the in-house asset management arm of the financial giant Prudential and Philip worked as a fund manager, although he was never one of the 'star managers' – rather someone who fundamentally just got on with the job.

A colleague who knew him when he moved to Deutsche Asset Management told the *Financial Times* that he was a 'steady Eddy' rather than a superstar, adding, 'He was not at the cutting edge of the City.' Perhaps this was just as well. Neither of the Mays was ever implicated in any way in the City scandals either then or now and after his wife entered frontline politics (possibly as a result of it), Philip left the money management side of things altogether and moved into client relationship, where his much-commented upon diplomatic skills were sometimes called into play to explain to a client why an investment had gone down instead of up. However, this was still to come and at first it was not clear whether a life in finance would be a stepping stone into a life in frontline politics as his wife's career in finance was to be, or a full-time end in itself, but at that point domestic issues were taking up all of his time. A year after graduation came the marriage and after that Philip needed to provide total support for his new wife as the tragedy unfurled itself. It was to be a while before life got back to normal.

The couple settled in south London and got on with what appeared to be an uneventful life, although the shocks of the previous few years were surely being felt. Both were progressing in their careers. In 1985, two years after leaving the Bank of England and after two years as a consultant for the Inter-Bank Research Organisation, Theresa took a job at the Association of Payment Clearing Services (APACs), which is about as exciting as it sounds and where she stayed until 1997, when she became an MP. It did, however, entail working with the banking industry in the UK and its relationship with the EU at a time when much of the continent was preparing to adopt the euro, which gave her a unique insight not only into what a disaster the euro was going to be but also the complexity involved in getting in or out of it. You could say it was a preparation of sorts for dealing with Brexit.

It was also the period when the industry was reforming CHAPS, the Clearing House Automated Payment System, which was established in February 1984 to offer same-day sterling fund transfers, and while there was nothing particularly ground-breaking about all this to an external observer, again it was a mark of Theresa's attention to detail and ability to grasp complex ideas that came through in her mastery of the role. The reform of CHAPS was another of the seismic shifts in the way the City did business in the 1980s, again with Theresa close at hand to observe exactly what was going on.

Indeed, on the CV she later prepared when applying to become an MP, she described this time as 'experience of negotiating for UK in Europe'. Calm, unflappable, sensible and level-headed – just as she is today – Theresa ended up as head of the European Affairs Unit and senior adviser on International Affairs, good solid achievements that were not going to frighten the horses. Some people pursue a City career to make a lot of money before going into politics; in Theresa's case, it was merely to provide a stable income while she began to look at what really interested her – on a local level, at least. She never seemed to be in it for the money; it was Philip who appeared to be happy with the more traditional type of City career.

In later years, talking of her time in the City, Theresa was keen to emphasise that this – administration – was the side she worked with and not the deal-making side which had led some to compare it unfavourably to a casino and a crooked one at that. Although the post-Big Bang City worked more efficiently than it had done previously, some old timers regretted the loss of the former culture of late starts, long lunches and four-day weekends, all of which were soon to be banished into the mists of time, and it was also the case that although insider trading was by now illegal, there was still scope for an ambitious young man (in those days they tended to be men) to twist the system to his advantage, not always within the bounds of legality.

Theresa would have been very aware of the darker side of the new way the City functioned, and as time wore on, other excesses, such as massive corporate pay at the top of the tree, would also alienate the public and fuel a certain degree of anger at corporate greed, one which it is to be imagined that the virtuous vicar's daughter would share. The 1980s was also a time of asset stripping, best exemplified in the 1987 film *Wall Street*, a practice by which one company would buy another and then dismantle it, selling all its component parts for far more than it had initially paid. Invariably large job losses ensued. Unemployment was rising anyway at the start of the 1980s when a highly turbulent decade in politics got well and truly under way.

But as the duo settled into their chosen careers and married life together, and as Theresa began to recover from the shock of losing her parents, the interest in politics that both had cultivated at Oxford started to sparkle again. Britain was changing, massively, and not just in the City. Margaret Thatcher had become the first female British Prime Minister in 1979 and her wish, expressed in a quote from St Francis of Assisi, 'Where there is discord, may we bring harmony,' was proving to be somewhat wide of the mark. Her initial and savage unpopularity had been sharply reversed with the unexpected Argentinian invasion of the Falkland Islands in 1982 and the subsequent triumph in the Falklands War, but while for some parts of the country she could do no wrong, for others she was the devil incarnate.

The Falklands War was swiftly followed by the 1984–85 miners' strike: this succeeded not merely in dividing the UK but also dividing actual families as some family members enthusiastically manned the barricades after the President of the National Union of Mineworkers, Arthur Scargill, called a national strike without a proper ballot of the members, while others thought it was unconstitutional and refused to strike. The BBC referred to it as 'the most bitter industrial dispute in

British history' and while the BBC can often justly be accused of bias against the Conservative Party, in this case they were almost certainly right. Dreadful scenes occurred across the country, with rallies turning violent, bitter clashes occurring on picket lines and finally the so-called 'Battle of Orgreave', in which police on horseback charged 5,000 rioting miners with terrible injuries on both sides.

In the midst of it all came the Brighton bombing on 12 October 1984, which took place during the Conservative Party Conference. While it was designed by the IRA to kill the Prime Minister and as much as her government as it could aim for, Mrs Thatcher herself escaped injury, although there were five fatalities and thirty-one people injured. Thatcher, as was to be expected, responded magnificently to the terror, beginning the conference at 9.30 a.m., as planned.

She had also planned on attacking Labour, then as now totally unelectable, but this clearly was the priority to be addressed: it was 'an attempt to cripple Her Majesty's democratically elected Government. That is the scale of the outrage in which we have all shared, and the fact that we are gathered here now – shocked, but composed and determined – is a sign not only that this attack has failed, but that all attempts to destroy democracy by terrorism will fail.' Her popularity ratings shot up again, to levels last seen during the Falklands War. An object lesson in how any statesman, male or female, should behave, it also earned her comparisons with Winston Churchill and an awareness that the country was now being led by one of the greatest prime ministers it had ever seen.

Yet still the miners' strike raged on . . . It was an extraordinary time to be living through, not least as the international perception of Britain was beginning to change. Margaret Thatcher enjoyed a famously good relationship with the American President Ronald Reagan, but as the shock of the recession of the Thatcher early years receded, it became apparent that Britain was changing, and very much for the better, with an energy in the air that had not been felt before. Britain was stirring, changing, perhaps, from a manufacturing economy to a service economy (and both Mays worked in the service industry) and above it all, Mrs Thatcher strode the scene like a colossus, continuing to divide feelings (including among her own party) in a way no politician had done for generations yet merely growing in stature. It was a very exciting time.

The Mays had already had some experience of politics, of course, both at Oxford and in Theresa's case as a child as well. Now they decided – both of them – to go into local politics and while this would be the full extent of Philip's engagement, the next few years provided a valuable learning curve for his wife's future career. For a start, both decided to delve into the local politics of south London where they were based, the Merton Conservatives: Philip rose to become the president of the Wimbledon Conservative Association – Wimbledon being part of Merton – followed by chairman of the London SW Euro-Constituency.

That, however, marked the end of it and despite the rumour that they had a Blair-style agreement in that whichever found a seat first would get the political career, there is no evidence that Philip ever actually looked for a seat. Comfortable in his City career as a fund manager, it appears that at around this time he decided to go no further. He did so 'for no other reason than that he had a different approach to life,' according to the couple's friend Alan Duncan: 'Theresa was prepared to step into the light of public gaze. Philip preferred to be more in the background. It's as simple as that.'

Certainly from that moment on, when they were still in their twenties, Philip stepped into the role of supportive husband as Theresa began her journey up the greasy pole. And just as she is so inevitably compared to Margaret Thatcher, who was at that point at her absolute indomitable height, so comparisons would come to be made between Philip and Denis Thatcher, who had been in the slightly less than enviable position of being the first male spouse to inhabit Number 10. The common consensus was that he had made a pretty good fist of it but no man had ever been forced to do so before (although in fairness, Britain also had a female monarch with an alpha-male husband, whose lot in life had been to play a supporting role) and Denis had come under a good deal of scrutiny to see whether he would crumble under the pressure of it all.

He didn't, of course, and in that he was almost certainly aided by the satirical magazine *Private Eye*, which ran a regular feature throughout Margaret Thatcher's time in office purporting to be letters from the Prime Minister's spouse. Entitled 'Dear Bill' – 'Bill' was never formally identified but was universally assumed to be the Conservative politician and *Daily Telegraph* editor Bill Deedes – many assumed the reactionary and frequently sozzled buffoon it portrayed to be the real Denis, which served only to create a frisson of affection around him.

As with Theresa and Margaret, while there were some similarities between Philip and Denis, it was by no means the whole picture. The similarities lay in the fact that both had successful careers, which was crucial, as both were called upon to put themselves second to their wives and only a man who is very comfortable in his own skin would have been able to do that. Both also somewhat sensibly avoided the Cherie Blair route of seeing themselves as political figures in their own right and thus liable to open their mouths and make fools of themselves as she so often did during the Blair years: 'Better keep your mouth shut and be thought a fool than open it and remove all doubt,' as Denis Thatcher once put it. Nor did either of them ever show the acquisitiveness displayed by Cherie and, after he stepped down, her husband too.

But in other areas they were very different. The public image of Denis as a bit of a toper was in fact entirely correct – famously he had a long list of names for tipples in the order in which they were taken as 'an opener, a brightener, a lifter, a large gin and tonic without the tonic, a snifter, a short, a snorter. And a snortorino, which more or less empties the bottle in one go' – whereas Philip, like his wife, was a creature of moderation, confining himself to the odd glass of wine.

It also seems that just as Theresa's views were more moderate than Margaret's, so too were Philip's slightly less eye-wateringly stringent than those of Denis, who was in reality far more to the right of the political spectrum than he ever publicly let on. And of course the Thatchers had children, unlike the Mays, something that would briefly play a large part in Theresa's election campaign to become party leader. By virtue of the fact she was a public figure, Theresa has been forced to speak out about this, something she would obviously rather have avoided, but Philip has never allowed his views on the subject to be known.

Theresa is not the only one who likes to keep her cards close to her chest.

6

A SHOWCASE OF
THE TALENTS

Theresa May, like everyone else in the UK, was following Margaret Thatcher's progress very closely, and now she began to make steps that would end up with her becoming an MP, an ambition she had harboured from the age of twelve. While the parents who had so encouraged her were sadly not around to see what their daughter would achieve, Theresa must have been thinking of them as she began to plan her way to the top. There are various routes into becoming an elected representative, including becoming a special adviser to a minister (which is what David Cameron, who at that point was living it up with the Bullingdon Club in Oxford, did), but Theresa chose the more traditional route of a spate in local government before fixing her gaze on the national stage.

In lots of ways it could be said that this is a better preparation for government: while many politicians are accused of being remote from the public, with the kind of career behind them that never really involved the real world, Theresa was to spend the best part of a decade dealing with local people and local issues. It was hard slog and not very glamorous, but it was to toughen her up still further for the challenges that lay ahead. Merton, the area in which she lived and got involved, was also an interesting place in which to serve an apprenticeship.

Though Merton might include the pretty London village of Wimbledon, with its grand mansions and common within its boundaries, along with the famous annual Grand Slam tennis tournament, it is nothing like the urbane Notting Hill and North Kensington from which Cameron and co would one day emerge. Merton lies quite a way south of the river and it is very suburban; the grand white stuccoed houses of Kensington and Chelsea are not reproduced out there, this is a place of red-brick terraced houses, road after road looking very much the same. Anyone who wanted to get a sense of its geographical layout could do worse than look at the television series, *The Bill* (1984–2010), much of which was filmed in the Merton districts of Mitcham and Colliers Wood, for this is suburbia in the raw. Tourists might visit attractive Wimbledon Village and the tennis tournament and perhaps even the local football team, but Merton is not on the list of London must-sees. It is supremely unflashy and as such an obvious place from which a politician like Theresa May might emerge. Somewhat more surprisingly, it was also the origin of a whole generation of British politicians who would go on to do very well, of which more below.

Theresa and Philip got in touch with their local Conservative Association to see how they could be of help. To begin with, Theresa went back to her childhood pastime of stuffing envelopes, pretty much de rigueur for anyone who wants to play a part in their local Conservative Association, but it wasn't long before she was taking on a much more active role. Local associations are split between those who simply want to volunteer their time and services – not only stuffing envelopes but also manning the fêtes, charity quizzes, speeches by local dignitaries, suppers, receptions, summer parties, balls, manning polling stations, supporting the local MP and so much more that makes up the life of the party – and those who are prepared to put themselves up for election to become councillors, representing the local people and fighting for their cause. As with national politics, the candidates must be chosen by the party and then submit themselves to the whim of the electorate, and Merton was one of those boroughs that swung between Tory and Labour. It might not have been competitive on the scale of national politics, but it was competitive just the same, and, of course, it was yet more training for what was to come.

In 1986, when she was not yet thirty, Theresa was elected as a councillor for Durnsford Ward in Wimbledon, with a majority of less than 100 in a Conservative-run council, and soon she was playing an even more active role in the Borough: she became chairman for education, a post held from 1988–90. She proved herself to be exactly what Theresa has always been: calm, unflashy and competent. And she was popular with the people of the area, who very much had the impression she was working hard on their behalf. Theresa was still working at APACs by day, but it was affording her the time to do her politics on the evenings and at weekends. Working as a local politician can be as much or as little work as the individual wants it to be: as a councillor, Theresa was obviously expected to show up for meetings and debates, but there are good councillors and bad councillors, just as there are good and bad MPs too.

She took her duties seriously, though, not least because she was now eyeing up another prize, the next step up the ladder, and was starting to plan how she would achieve her long-term ambition to become an MP. And her work translated into votes. In 1990, the year that Margaret Thatcher was stabbed in the back by her MPs, Theresa was re-elected. This time around she got her majority up to 150, although there was a Labour majority on the council, and so she got her first taste of politics in opposition. She became deputy group leader and housing spokesman from 1992–94. Perhaps unsurprisingly, those with whom she worked at the time speak well of her.

Councillor David Williams had been on the London

Borough of Merton for a dozen years when Theresa came on board and he was very impressed by her. She was still extremely young and yet showing all the rigour in approaching her brief that was to be on display time and again. 'Theresa was someone who did her homework,' he told *International Business Times* in July 2016. 'She had high expectations of people that they take decisions based only on information, and she was hard on herself, as well as her opposition. She took decisions with her head, even though she had a warm heart. She was also a very good ward councillor. We used to make fun of her for a voicemail message she left for her ward constituents. She would say, "Your call is very important to me, please leave me a message and I will try and get back to you." It's common nowadays but back then it wasn't. We all thought it was a bit over the top but she truly meant it, and it showed how much her constituents meant to her.'

This time on Merton Council was not just a preparation for future office, it was also the start of a loose-knit power base that in later years became known as the 'Wimbledon Set'. Famously un-cliquey, Theresa doesn't hobnob with colleagues just for the sake of it and when she came to be elected as an MP, she didn't spend time schmoozing in the Commons tea room, but she has always had a close-knit set of associates and the formation of a group of people who, to use the vernacular, watched each other's backs. For example, a few years later Chris Grayling also became a Merton councillor, in his case, for Hillside Ward, and it was the same Chris Grayling who was later Theresa's campaign manager when she bid for the party leadership and whom she then made Secretary of State for Transport.

Something similar was to happen a few miles across town, north of the river in Notting Hill, a decade or so thence. It was in that affluent enclave that David Cameron, George Osborne and Michael Gove would plan their takeover of the Tory Party, but in their case the tone was different. Cameron and Osborne came from money and privilege (admittedly, Michael Gove does not, but he always came across as something as an outsider compared to the other two); when asked why he should become prime minister, Cameron famously replied, 'Well, I think I'd be rather good at it.' This was a set of people who even now had been brought up to rule and there was a certain expectation that the glittering prizes would drop into their laps. The group of people trudging around far less glamorous Merton, putting election leaflets through letter boxes, debating on what to do with the local schools, was not like that at all. Theresa May and Chris Grayling had similar backgrounds: both were grammar-school educated, followed by Oxbridge, then a career in the outside world before they entered politics. Neither of them thought they had a divine right to rule, both worked hard for it, and they started back then.

Local politics was teaching Theresa a lot: she was not one for the raised voice but by the time she got to the Commons, she had perfected the 'death stare' that was capable of freezing a grown man at fifty paces. She didn't need to learn the art of debating – she had already done that at Oxford – but now she was seeing at first hand the need, at whatever level, to negotiate and compromise. Moreover, her time on Merton Council gave some foretaste as to the knockabouts and blows she would be expected to be a party to once in mainstream politics, for while she might have taken a personal interest in the people she was serving as councillor, that did not mean she had a smooth ride.

Unpopular decisions that were made under Theresa's watch included closing a local primary school, which landed her in very hot water with parents, fury from the Labour Party when cuts were announced to the education budget and further hostility when she opposed Wimbledon FC's move to Wimbledon Greyhound Stadium. She was fast developing an extremely thick skin, and of course at that point Philip was still involved with his own brand of local politics and the two of them, now becoming increasingly aware that they were unlikely ever to have children, were forming an ever-closer unit. Indeed Philip was to become one of the few people Theresa could ever entirely rely on to have her best interests at heart and she was also able to use him as a sounding board.

Theresa's one and slightly surprising non-conformist streak came then in the clothes that she wore. This most down-to-earth of women, this sober personality, this hard-working and unflashy career woman, seemed to allow herself just one outlet in which she was allowed to be a little more flamboyant and that was in her wardrobe. Photographs taken at the time show a typical 1980s power-suited look, nothing too shocking or controversial there: Theresa can be seen with a short bob, bright red shoulder-padded suit and slash of red lipstick. Even then she managed to use clothes to stand out, her scarlet appearance in sharp contrast to the sombre-suited men and women surrounding her. But in marked contrast to the clothes is the expression: Theresa looks serious, she has weighty matters on her mind. And so it has always been. A few years later, when the nation first became aware of her liking for leopard-skin kitten heels, she was wearing them when she was giving a sharp dressing-down to her party. The clothes might have hinted at a lighter side, never exhibitionist but certainly no bluestocking, but heaven help anyone who didn't take seriously what she actually had to say.

But back then kitten heels were a thing of the future and in her determination to get on with the job in hand Theresa was even well thought of by the opposition. Councillor Philip Jones was a Labour man on Merton Council during Theresa's period in situ and spoke positively about her despite their clashes at the time: 'We all saw her as one of the more competent Tory councillors at the time. She made a positive contribution to the area and was quite a lively character,' he told *International Business Times* after Theresa became Prime Minister in July 2016. 'When I was chair of the environment committee, I remember her demanding my resignation. But I don't really remember what it was about.

I think, considering the alternatives, that the Conservatives picked the best person.'

Faint praise perhaps, but still a long way from the bitterness that characterises so many other political relationships, and with more than a hint of respect.

In later years, this experience was to garner Theresa a lot of respect. Local politics can be quite as gruelling as the national variety and the general feeling was that she – and some of the others in this set – had done a hard slog to get to where they were. It was also noted in many quarters that although Labour took over the council for the second term Theresa was there, she herself managed to increase her own majority. 'Both Theresa May and Chris Grayling took the hard road,' John Elvidge, who was leader of Merton's Conservatives from 1988–90, told the *IBT*. 'They both survived that school of hard knocks. Local politics at that time was very difficult, especially dealing with budget challenges. She survived when we lost the council in the 1990 election because she'd learnt to be such a good ward councillor. And she was, as you see her now – very balanced, and very lucid.'

And very focused on the bigger picture too.

Yet still Merton continued to punch far above its weight in terms of the quality of people it attracted on to the local council, who would go on to greater things. Other councillors included Tariq Ahmad, later Lord Ahmad, someone else who knew he wanted to go into politics from a very young age. Tariq came from the area and was educated at a local comprehensive; there was certainly no whiff of privilege there. He too had an extensive career in the real world before he went into politics, working for NatWest, AllianceBernstein L.P. and Sucden Financial, among others. He became a councillor in Wimbledon, vice chair of the Conservative Party itself and, after entering the Lords, a colleague of Chris Grayling at Transport.

Another Wimbledon whizz-kid was Stephen Hammond, who was educated at King Edward VI School, Southampton, a grammar school that became independent in 1978, followed by Queen Mary University of London, and who also did a stint in the City, in his case Dresdner Kleinwort Benson, then Commerzbank Securities Limited, before becoming a Merton councillor for the Ward of Village, Wimbledon, becoming Wimbledon's MP in 2005. He too worked at Transport.

Maria Miller tried to get elected to Merton Council and when she missed out by one vote, she followed Philip's example and became chair of Wimbledon Conservatives. She went on to become MP for Basingstoke and held several ministerial positions before being forced to resign from the Cabinet in 2014 for over-claiming expenses (equality between the sexes had clearly hit the Tories in less favourable ways, too). Sarah Newton, MP for Truro and Falmouth and a former assistant whip in the Treasury, and also Suzanne Evans of UKIP, all served on Merton Council – in Evans's case, as a Conservative, before she moved over to UKIP.

'It is truly extraordinary how many of those councillors

back then have risen up so highly,' Harry Cowd, Leader of the Merton Conservatives when Theresa arrived in 1986, told the *IBT* after Mrs May became PM in 2016. 'Merton is a comparatively small borough. I think it could partly be how the local party operated back then, going out as unpaid volunteers and speaking to everyone. It was interesting to watch Theresa go into Downing Street. She seems to be the same as how she operated as a councillor. She worked very hard. She's come up through a different line compared to Cameron and I think it's helpful to have served on the ground first. Merton is a mixed community and Theresa was always able to bridge the different communities.'

Another thing that every single member of the above list had in common is that they all had jobs in the non-political sphere before turning their attention first to Merton Council and then the Houses of Parliament. Many worked in the City, but not all: Maria Miller, for example, worked in advertising and marketing, and Sarah Newton, while starting in various financial firms, served as a director for Age Concern and made the problems of an ageing society one of her specialist subjects in other ways as well. Of course this concentration of the talents in one small area could be for more pragmatic reasons, too. Apart from isolated hotspots like Wimbledon Village, house prices in Merton are a fraction of what they are in Kensington and Chelsea and Notting Hill and all these clever, able people, who were so keen to get into politics, did not have the trust funds behind them that a rather better-off set of Tory cronies would one day have. They lived in the less privileged areas because they simply couldn't afford the huge sums necessary to get them into the best postcodes. If nothing else it meant that they really did get to see how most people lived.

When Theresa May became Prime Minister, she was the first to have had this background as a local councillor since Sir John Major, who also famously came from a considerably less well-off background than a good many of his peers. Sir John took over after the defenestration of Margaret Thatcher in 1990 and while he will never go down in history as one of the greats, he was personable enough and also gave the impression of having some idea of what it is like to make your way through life without a parental fortune in the background. And he was keen to talk about the huge value of having spent time in local politics too.

'I wouldn't have missed the few years I was a Lambeth councillor for anything,' he said in a 1992 interview. 'It was one of the best learning schools in politics and in, I think as well, life that one could possibly have. You had almost every sort of problem to examine. People with all sorts of ambitions, some of which could be realised, some of which couldn't. You had a population mix of the most extraordinary kind. A large number of people in often very great difficulty.'

Although Theresa is often spoken of as an ice queen, she too has a far more personable side than is widely mentioned and people found her to be kind and helpful as well. Like every

MP, she was to hold surgeries in which she met constituents and discussed their problems; she took these duties seriously. And her interest in the people she was representing also started at a local level. These were also the people she was addressing when she made her speech on becoming PM.

Although her fellow councillors could have had no idea quite how successful the forthright young politician in their midst would become, Theresa made enough of an impression to be talked of even in the years before she got into Parliament and her name was often used subsequently to encourage others who were interested in politics to sign up. Merton Council in particular continued to boast of the association: in literature put out, asking people to get involved, Theresa's name came up repeatedly. The local press continued to report on her dealings, too, and when she reached Number 10 there was no shortage of comment on where she had begun.

'It's remarkable when you think about it,' Merton councillor James Holmes, who campaigned with May as she sought her first parliamentary seat in 1992, told the *IBT*. 'There's a lot of the Wimbledon people – this Wimbledon set – who have now risen to high office after serving as councillors in Merton. I think Theresa's whole approach as Prime Minister will be quite different to Cameron's. She was very hard-working as a councillor. She wasn't someone interested in courting personality coverage, but instead just wanted to get on with the job.'

But before she could do so, of course, she had to get elected. And so Theresa, secure in her personal life, already beginning to get noticed in her public life, took the next step en route to Downing Street: the time had come to look for a parliamentary seat.

7

CLIMBING THE GREASY POLE

There are several steps on the road to getting elected to Parliament, some of them a requirement, others less formal, and there are now various organisations, one of them co-founded by Theresa May herself, to give women a helping hand. In the early 1990s, no such help existed. Of course Margaret Thatcher (who had had quite an effort to get into Parliament) never had any additional help either and someone as pragmatic and indeed talented as Theresa would simply have to get on with the job, but it was clearly a memory that stayed with the future Prime Minister because it was something she was to help rectify.

The first requirement to becoming a Tory MP was to get on the Approved List of candidates, which entailed applying to the Candidates Department and if successful submitting to a day-long assessment by the Parliamentary Assessment Board (PAB), which consists of MPs and senior Party volunteers. Years later, there was to be a huge row over one of Theresa's closest advisers failing to make this list but at the time she breezed through. That much was laid down in the rules; the next steps were more informal. In both the main political parties, but particularly so in the case of the Tories, formidable election-winning machine that they are, it is often, though not always, expected that the newly approved candidate will first fight an unwinnable seat. Those who don't tend to be the dreaded special advisers, who have already served their political masters well and so are deemed worthy of an early reward.

By the time Theresa started looking around in earnest for a seat, Margaret Thatcher had been gone for some years and a period of Tory Party infighting was about to commence that would go on for over a decade. Nor were women in a particularly good position vis-à-vis the Conservative Party. Mrs Thatcher had already shown that a woman could do the top job and then some, but the number of female MPs was still tiny, especially so in the Tories. When, against all expectation, John Major won the 1992 General Election, thereby paving the way for Tony Blair and the disastrous New Labour project, as well as allowing his own MPs to rip themselves and their party to shreds for years, only 60 MPs who took their seats were women, comprising just 9.2 per cent of the whole. Of these, 20 were Conservatives and 37 were Labour. Both parties were concerned about these low numbers and by the 1992 General Election Labour had insisted there was at least one female candidate on each of its shortlists.

In 1997, it went further still.

With Tony Blair now in charge, no stranger to an eye-catching initiative that would look good in the headlines no matter what the long-term consequences might be, Labour imposed all-women shortlists on half of all winnable seats with the goal of getting over 100 women to become Labour MPs. It worked. In 1997, 120 women were elected to Parliament (still only 18.2 per cent of the whole), of which 101 were Labour and 13 (including Theresa May) were Conservative. It was a pretty wretched showing, and even as recently as 2015 there were still only 29 female Tory MPs out of the 191 as a whole, who themselves do not yet constitute one-third of the House.

There are many theories as to why this should be, the most likely being that it is exceptionally difficult both to bring up a family and excel in an exceptionally difficult job. (It is also said that women don't like the bear pit atmosphere of the House of Commons although anyone who has seen both of Britain's female Prime Ministers wiping the floor with the opposition might have their doubts about that.) But as the Labour experience showed, all-female shortlists are not the solution. Apart from the patronising nature of the photographs of the egregious Tony Blair smirking as he was flanked by the women who came to be known as 'Blair's Babes' in the wake of the 1997 Labour electoral landslide, it meant that a lot of second-raters were able to get into the Mother of All Parliaments, and one of them was Jacqui Smith. Jacqui was a predecessor of Theresa's as Home Secretary, but that is about the only thing the two women have in common.

Smith lasted just two years in the role and made herself a laughing stock when it emerged that her husband had claimed for a porn film during the MPs' expenses row. She also looked ridiculous when she claimed that a spare room in her sister's house was her 'main residence' and all-female party list or no, lost her seat in the 2010 General Election. If ever there was a person who illustrated that artificially tipping the scales produces mediocrities, it is Jacqui Smith. Then there is also the problem that even if an outstanding female candidate gets through, there will always be the suspicion that she only hit the big time because she was given preferential treatment ahead of a man.

Not that this was an issue for Theresa May back in the early 1990s when she first started putting out feelers to see what would be available. It is a cliché, but nonetheless true, that the people who inhabit the selection committees of Tory local parties and above all, the women, are (or perhaps 'were') looking for a man of a very particular type: white, middle-class, professional and married, preferably with a few children. The spousal element is important: MPs' wives tended to live in the constituency while their husbands spent the week in London. They would devote themselves to local activities such as bring-and-buy sales and generally spread an aura of domestic contentment. It tended, in fact, to be an illustration of the 'different spheres' that both sexes were once said to inhabit – men out in the big, wide world and women in the home.

Of course there had been exceptions, many of them and not just on the Conservative benches. Labour, before it became obsessed with image under Blair and before it imploded in recent years, produced some outstanding women, including the likes of Baroness Betty Boothroyd and Barbara Castle. But the fact is that it was and remains more difficult to make it in politics if you are a woman and that is what Theresa was now determined to do.

After casting her net around, she was picked as a candidate to stand in North West Durham, a constituency in which most of the population lived in former mining and steel towns and which had been solidly Labour for decades. Its sitting MP in 1992 was Hilary Armstrong, who had been there since 1987 and who was to become a government minister and chief whip under Tony Blair. Theresa didn't have a chance of winning, and neither did the Liberal Democrat candidate, one Tim Farron, then a twenty-one-year-old Newcastle University student, who would also go on to become the leader of his party a couple of decades later.

Then again, no one thought the Tories stood much of a chance of winning at all. John Major had seemingly come out of nowhere to become Prime Minister in 1990 after his colleagues destroyed Margaret Thatcher (maintaining a remarkably low profile in the turmoil surrounding her political assassination, a tactic Theresa herself would employ to great effect in the referendum campaign) but the vicious Tory infighting that was to dominate the party until the election of David Cameron as its leader had already begun, and after thirteen years the general feeling was that the country needed a change.

Major had cauterised the wound created by the fiercely unpopular imposition of the Community Charge, better known as the 'Poll Tax', by getting rid of it, but there was disillusionment in the air and the early nineties saw a tired Conservative Party, rather than the energetic vote winner of the 1980s seemingly limping through the motions. Nonetheless, a combination of public mistrust of the Labour Party and its then leader Neil Kinnock's triumphalism meant that the country decided it was better the devil you know and voted the Tories back in. Had they not done so, history might have been very different – Neil Kinnock would have been a disastrous prime minister, the Tories would have been back in power in 1997, and Tony Blair and New Labour would never have happened – but they did. And so the Tories rounded on one another and started to self-destruct in earnest, in full glare of the limelight. The full extent of the massive bitterness unleashed by the fall of Mrs Thatcher was only now beginning to hit home.

This didn't make much difference to Theresa, who would not have expected to win anyway. She did what she could, submitting a CV that listed not only her various roles in local government but also the fact that she was a member of Surrey County Cricket Club, a Fellow of the Royal Geographical Society and that her specialised knowledge included education, local government and Europe. She polled 12,747 votes, 27.6 per cent of the total, a fall of 0.8 per cent on the previous Tory candidate, Derek Iceton, against Hilary Armstrong's 22,947 votes, 50.9 per cent of the total. But, and far more pertinently, it was widely perceived that Theresa had made a very good fist of fighting a hopeless seat. It also gave her an insight into what the people of the north-east thought of the Conservative Party – in the wake of the coal and steel closures in the area there was almost certainly not a place in the UK better able to make it clear that not everyone thought they were the saviours of the nation and it might well have informed one of Theresa's most famous speeches, the one that brought her to widespread public attention when she became the Conservative Party chairman a decade thence. It was the one in which she pointed out that 'nice' was not the first word that sprang to some lips when the Conservatives came to mind.

Hilary, now Baroness Armstrong, gave her own take on it after Theresa became Prime Minister in 2016. 'She bought a house in Lanchester when she was selected, and she would meet at Tory supporters' houses and they would have tea and cakes,' she told the *Northern Echo*. 'She didn't do any public events or attend hustings.

'I met her for the first time at the count. She was very thin and wore a Thatcher-style bright blue suit with a short skirt, and she was very composed – she knew she wasn't going to win, so her campaign was to maintain the core vote and she concentrated on Weardale and Lanchester. She was doing it to demonstrate she could do it, and to gain exposure to Tory shire northern people, and I am sure that has stood her in good stead.'

Baroness Armstrong went on to make the pertinent point that it would also have exposed Theresa to a different kind of Tory voter, not just those who lived in the prosperous south. 'I know that she'd fought a really effective campaign to try to secure the Tory vote,' she told the *Global North East & Yorkshire News*. 'And what she had done was have house meetings really in the houses of Tory supporters, where they would invite half a dozen friends and then go and meet with them and talk with them and it was actually very successful because the Tory vote in that election only went down by about 50 votes [*sic* – it was 38]. And that's what will have done her in good stead. She will now know what that sort of Tory person thinks. What they believe. What motivates them. What keeps them as Tory voters.

'She knew that she was never going to win the seat but she nonetheless had a very effective campaign. I wouldn't say I spotted her as a future prime minister but I did spot her as someone who was going to be very determined, clearly focused on what she wanted to do. I knew she'd be able to see her house and pay for the campaign so she planned it all very well. It is an advantage that she's been on the north east. But what they want is someone who treats them fairly and gives them opportunity. We have huge challenges in the north east. We need to grow our economy in the north east. People need to feel better off. The recession hit the north-east hard but we've done well in manufacturing, but she's got to get us a good deal in Europe so that we don't lose that manufacturing base.'

That was also a pertinent point: hostility towards the EU was greatest in the poorer areas of the UK, where the influx of immigrants was widely perceived to have driven down wages, deprived locals of employment and put an intolerable strain on social services and Theresa, from the time that she spent there, would have been more aware than many front-bench Tories of what the mood in certain parts of the country was really like.

But that was for the future. Back in the past, having put on a good show, Theresa was on the search for a second winnable seat, something with which she was not rewarded. However, what happened next also stood her in good stead. She was selected to fight Barking and in 1994, two years after John Major's surprise election victory, with tension in the Tory ranks growing, a by-election was held in Barking. This was following the death of the incumbent MP, Josephine 'Jo' Richardson, who had held the seat since 1974, and the constituency itself had been solid Labour since it was created in 1945. In 1992 Jo had increased her majority by 6,000 so there was no chance at all of Theresa being elected and both she and the Conservatives knew this. In the event she was to lose pretty badly as the country's discontent with the Major administration began to show through in the polls. Labour chose the Leader of the Islington Borough Council, Margaret Hodge, as their candidate, while the Lib Dems opted for the twenty-one-year-old Garry White.

The world was different back then, too. In South Africa, this was the year when Nelson Mandela became the country's first black president; back in Britain the eccentric Screaming Lord Sutch, founder of the Official Monster Raving Loony Party, was campaigning for a 'poop scoop' scheme to clear up dog mess (and, like a lot of his party's proposals, seems extremely sensible in retrospect). Barking, in east London, is not a wealthy area. In recent years it has benefited from the 2012 Olympics, but with high numbers of social housing and low-paid workers, it was never going to welcome a Tory candidate. In more recent years it has been targeted, pretty unsuccessfully, by the BNP.

But once again Theresa put on a good show. Although she knew it was hopeless, she did her best, knocking on doors in a vain attempt to get the voters out for the Tories. She campaigned on local issues, such as bringing a rail link to Barking riverside, but to no avail.

'Tory candidates who want to be MPs go for seats like Barking, where it would be a miracle if they won, as a testing ground,' explained Brian Cook, who had been a local Conservative councillor at the time.

Theresa also highlighted the inadequacies of the Labour-run council, particularly in the area of schools, was very tough on the subject of crime and reminded voters that it was the Tories who had brought in the legislation to allow them to buy their council houses. Right from the get-go, however, there were ominous warnings that she could end up in third place.

But Theresa was game. She tried to 'make herself look like an Essex girl, or what she assumed we looked like,' local councillor Jeannette Alexander, who later campaigned for her, told the *Barking and Dagenham Post*. 'One time she had very blonde hair [and a] short cerise-coloured suit. Within a couple of weeks of coming third in Barking, she wore long skirts and pearls, ready for the next seat she tried for.' Ironically, she and Margaret Hodge had more in common than the onlooker might have thought: both had a history in local government and Hodge, if anything, came from a considerably more urbane area of London than did Theresa. Merton is not a sophisticated place, whereas Margaret's home patch was Islington, which is the area Blair and his cronies emerged from, close to the bustling centre, replete with chi-chi restaurants, antiques arcades and the Sadler's Wells Theatre to boot. It is arguable that Theresa would have understood the concerns of Barking far more than Hodge ever could.

However it was not to be. The seat would not have been

winnable for a Tory candidate under the most propitious circumstances and these were anything but. John Major might have won the election but that was pretty much the end of his winning streak: from there on in it was one disaster after another. The Tories had scarcely been re-elected before they suffered the shock of Black Wednesday when, on 16 September 1992, the UK was forced to leave the European Exchange Rate Mechanism (ERM), a humiliation from which they would never recover. Major's personal popularity was plummeting; he had been overheard on microphone calling the ministers who were opposed to the implementation of the Maastricht Treaty 'bastards' and then to cap it all, in 1993 he launched his risible 'Back to Basics' campaign, allegedly about matters concerning the economy but taken by just about everyone as pertaining to private morality. And so the cupboard doors opened and the skeletons came tumbling out.

David Mellor, the Secretary of State for National Heritage, had been having an affair with Antonia de Sancha, an actress, and accepted hospitality from the daughter of a prominent member of the Palestine Liberation Organisation (PLO) and was forced to resign in1992. Meanwhile the Tory peer, Malcolm Sinclair, Earl of Caithness, found himself in the news when it was revealed that his wife had committed suicide after rumours he'd had an affair, the Tory MP David Ashby was outed by his wife as gay after sharing a bed with a man (in those days it was still extremely rare to be outwardly gay in public life) and Minister for Environment and Countryside Tim Yeo, who had spoken out against single parents, was forced to resign after it was revealed he had a love child.

Then, in 1994, shortly before the Barking by-election the MP Stephen Milligan was found dead in bizarre circumstances after an act of autoerotic asphyxiation and while the 'cash for questions' scandal wouldn't erupt until later in the year, the public was already feeling extremely disillusioned with its elected representatives. Add to that Arms-to-Iraq, in which government officials were accused of encouraging British businesses to supply arms to Iraq during the 1980s Iran–Iraq War despite a trade embargo and, admittedly yet to come and so not directly influencing Barking, the MP Jonathan Aitken wielding 'the sword of truth and the trusty shield of British fair play' and subsequently being found guilty of perjury and perverting the course of justice and much, much more and you had a government in meltdown.

John Major had totally lost any authority he might once have wielded and he failed to regain it even after his resignation in 1995 and, somewhat unusually, forcing a leadership challenge on himself. He might have been re-elected to lead the party but that was the last election he was going to win. The Tory press had turned on him, and within the party the act of matricide committed against Mrs Thatcher was, if anything, taking on greater significance than ever. She would never have run such a shambles of a government, was the thinking of the supporters who had never forgiven the plotters who toppled her, some, including Michael Heseltine and Kenneth Clarke, now holding senior positions in government. Thatcher had never lost an election and a large proportion of the party, including huge swathes of the grassroots, believed she should have been allowed to fight the 1992 one. She hadn't, and this was the result.

All in all it wasn't exactly the best moment to extol the virtues of the Conservative Party in a Labour-held area and Barking was just one of the by-elections held at the time that spelled it out that come the next General Election, the Tories were headed for a serious defeat. And so, when Theresa May comprehensively lost in Barking, pushed into a humiliating third place after Margaret Hodge, who polled 72.1 per cent of the vote, and the Lib Dem Garry White, it was seen not so much as a wipeout for her as for John Major. This was not a personal judgement on Theresa, more a poke in the eye at Major's shambolic, exhausted, calamity-prone government.

The papers didn't hold back: 'Blue murder!' shrieked the *Daily Star*. Theresa took it on the chin, but then she always did. To a Tory keen to be going places, the 1990s were an ordeal, although at that stage no one anticipated the scale of the 1997 defeat. But the local organisations were keen to find candidates who would not have sex scandals queuing up to be discovered, who had kept their fingers out of the till, their snouts out of the trough and not encouraged dodgy arms deals with the Middle East nor had children with their mistresses while extolling the virtues of the nuclear family. To put it bluntly, they wanted candidates who were respectable, capable and had a chance of pulling the party back together again.

Theresa had now fought two hopeless seats and acquitted herself well. In the process she had had to endure the microscopic examination of the national press that all politicians must endure. Not a comfortable experience, certainly not at the beginning, and all that anyone had been able to find out about her was that she was happily married, liked cooking and followed the cricket. Her true mettle was not yet entirely obvious: it would take entry into the Commons and her performance in the party before it would emerge that Theresa May might turn out to be one of the greats.

But she herself had had enough of fighting for useless seats and she'd served her time now; she was due a political prize. Her personal circumstances were right: she'd laboured in a good job but would be happy to give it up, her personal life was rock solid and she had wanted to be an MP all her life. And so, with Philip's encouragement, Theresa began looking for a seat she could actually win, one that would get her into the Commons and get her career on track.

She was to find such a seat and indeed manage to become an MP after five years of trying. What she didn't know, what she couldn't possibly know, was 1997 was the worst single year in living memory to become a Conservative MP. She was not the only member of that fresh intake, but many others who were elected into Parliament at that time, shining hopes for the country and with a great future predicted for them, went on to fall by the wayside, forgotten and discredited. With the Cameron and Osborne takeover of the party, many were also to be passed over on age grounds, opportunities lost that would once have been open to them. The stupidity, arrogance and recklessness of the Tories who had brought down Margaret Thatcher didn't only destroy her, they made it impossible for a whole subsequent generation of MPs who entered Parliament years after her fall to have the career they might have done. But their number didn't include Theresa May. The challenges she faced would have finished many a lesser man or woman and indeed, in many cases they did. But for Theresa, a whole new future was about to open up.

The then Home Secretary arrives for a Cabinet meeting at No. 10 Downing Street, September 2010. *(© Fiona Hanson / PA Archive/Press Association Images)*

Top left: The chairman (as she preferred to be called) of the Conservative Party with its leader, the 'hapless Iain Duncan Smith', leaving a 'strategy meeting' for Tory MPs in May 2003. *(© Matthew Fearn / PA Archive/Press Association Images)*

Top right: Theresa and Philip May arrive at St Paul's Cathedral for the funeral of Lady Thatcher, 17 April 2013. *(© Bogdan Maran / AP/Press Association Images)*

Bottom left: Where Are They Now 1? – The Home Secretary on the government front bench with the then Chancellor, George Osborne, September 2015. Less than a year later, she sacked him. *(© PA / PA Archive/Press Association Images)*

Bottom right: Where Are They Now 2? – Seated near Michael Gove, on Eric Pickles's left, after five Birmingham schools had been placed in special administration in the wake of the 'Trojan Horse' inquiry which, as Education Secretary, Gove had instigated. It caused a serious rift between him and the Home Secretary, and he too would later be sacked from government.

(© PA Wire / PA Archive/Press Association Images)

Top left: 'I was told I couldn't deport Abu Qatada, but I flew to Jordan and negotiated the treaty that got him out of Britain for good.' The radical Islamist cleric is driven away after being refused bail at the Special Immigration Appeals Commission in London, 17 April 2012. He was deported in July the following year. (*© Matt Dunham / AP/Press Association Images*)

Top right: The Home Secretary visits the remains of the Sony Distribution Centre in Enfield, destroyed in the riots of August 2011. She had been on holiday when the rioting started, but returned immediately.

(*© Lewis Whyld / PA Archive/Press Association Images*)

Bottom: Where Are They Now 3? – Boris Johnson's hopes of succeeding David Cameron as Tory leader ended when Michael Gove decided to stand. After he withdrew from the contest, salvation for the former Mayor of London came from an unlikely quarter when the new Prime Minister appointed him Foreign Secretary on 13 July 2016. (*© John Stillwell / PA Archive/Press Association Images*)

Top: The media's perennial obsession with Mrs May's footwear is well illustrated here, as she listens to David Cameron at a press conference in October 2009. At the time, she was Shadow Work and Pensions Secretary.

(© *Tim Ireland / PA Archive/Press Association Images*)

Bottom: Coalition Cabinet – from left to right: Nick Clegg, Deputy Prime Minister and leader of the Liberal Democrats; David Cameron, Prime Minister; William Hague, Foreign Secretary; and Theresa May, Home Secretary, during a meeting of the National Security Council in the Cabinet Room at 10 Downing Street, 5 July 2010. (© *Peter Macdiarmid / PA Archive/Press Association Images*)

Top: Theresa May officially announces her decision to stand for the leadership of the Conservative Party at Austin Court in Birmingham, 11 July 2016.

(© *Chris Radburn / PA Wire/Press Association Images*)

Bottom: The Home Secretary makes a statement outside the Palace of Westminster after she won the votes of 199 Tory MPs, meaning that she would be on the ballot paper for the Conservative leadership vote.

(© *Matt Crossick / Matt Crossick/Empics Entertainment*)

Top: The candidates for the leadership of the Conservative Party before the first ballot. From left to right: Liam Fox, Theresa May, Stephen Crabb, Andrea Leadsom, Michael Gove. For complicated reasons, the contest would come down to a two-horse race between May and Leadsom.

(© *PA / PA Wire/Press Association Images*

Bottom left: Theresa May formally launches her leadership campaign at the Royal United Services Institute, London, 30 June 2016.

(© *Stefan Rousseau / PA Wire/Press Association Images*

Bottom right: Andrea Leadsom announces that she is quitting the leadership contest, leaving Theresa May as the sole candiadate, 11 July 2016. Among other reasons, Leadsom's reference, however oblique, to her rival's childlessness was to cost her dearly.

(© *AP / Press Association Images*

Top: By tradition, before assuming office the new Prime Minister must be invited to form a government by the monarch. Theresa May at an audience with HM the Queen at Buckingham Palace on 13 July 2016.

Bottom left: The UK's second woman prime minister makes a speech outside No. 10 Downing Street after her audience with the Queen.

Bottom right: To the applause of the assembled staff, Theresa May enters No. 10, followed by her husband of many years, Philip May.

The Rt Hon. Theresa May, MP, and her husband and chief supporter outside the door of No. 10 on the day she assumed office. She faces an arduous task, but there can be no doubting her courage, determination and commitment.

8

NEW GIRL

As the 1997 General Election approached, a mood for change was in the air. The Conservatives had been in power for eighteen years, effecting an astonishing change in British culture and society, dragging Britain out of the morass it had been in as 'the sick man of Europe' and empowering everyone including the working classes through its policy of selling off council houses and mass privatisations. The power of the unions had been smashed, national morale restored through the Falklands War, and Britain was once again definably a world power, able to hold her place on the global stage.

But all those progressions had been made under Margaret Thatcher and despite managing to keep the economy on track, one of the few real boasts it could make, the John

Major government had been a dismal affair. Weak leadership, constant plotting and attempts to undermine him and an utter absence of eye-catching policies – to this day some Tories wince when reminded of the 'cones hotline' (a telephone number for the public to use to report apparently pointless traffic cones on roads and enquire about roadworks), Black Wednesday and a myriad other crises to say nothing of the continuing anger about the treatment of Mrs Thatcher that had led the public to shun the so-called 'natural party of government'. They would almost certainly have lost the General Election anyway, but their plight was compounded by the fact that Tony Blair, Gordon Brown and Alastair Campbell had managed to take over the opposition party, branding it 'New Labour', and imposed a discipline on their own party combined with promises of a brighter future for everyone else that was memorably described by the journalist Ann Leslie as 'Stalinism for the parliamentary party and aromatherapy for the rest of us'.

No one in recent memory has fallen further in public opinion than Tony Blair, but back then, he was the master of all he surveyed. Personable, with a young family and anxious to reassure the country that he was the opposite of the hard left socialists who had tried to take over his party a decade previously (and would do so again), it seemed he could do no wrong. The grin that has become so strained in recent years was bright and switched on, the warmongering, the avariciousness, still lay ahead. The public was charmed by him, the business community felt safe with him . . . Blair promised a new future; a new outlook.

One of John Major's final acts of stupidity as Prime Minister boosted Blair's popularity even more: he sanctioned an ad that came to be known as 'demon eyes', a picture of a beaming Tony Blair with the eyes of a psychotic madman imposed over his face and the tagline, 'New Labour, New Danger'. No one (or at least not the majority of the public) suspected that Blair might not be the 'pretty straight sort of guy' he proclaimed himself to be in a BBC interview November 1997, and so this advertisement appeared to be so gratuitously spiteful that it completely rebounded on the perpetrators by giving him the sympathy vote on top of everything else.

No one seriously thought the Tories could win in 1997. That they had done so in 1992 took everyone by surprise, but their standing in the polls had collapsed since then. Wiser heads knew they were preparing for a rout, although no one was prepared for the scale of it either. It was an interesting time to become a Tory MP.

But Theresa May knew she was about to become exactly that. She had at last been picked for a safe seat, Maidenhead in Berkshire, and she and Philip were now resident in a charming village in the constituency, Sonning, which is where George and Amal Clooney now have their UK base. She had got there on the back of some very hard slog, not special treatment, and she was proud of it: 'I became a candidate on my merits,' she told *The Times* about ten days before the 1 May 2016 election. 'I have no burning ambition to promote women's parliamentary rights.' As a matter of fact she did, though not through a quota system, but it was probably a good idea to play it down.

Theresa's merits were already shining through pretty clearly, however. That same *Times* article quoted Emma Hobbs, who was on the panel in the local Conservative Party who chose her as their MP-to-be: 'When Theresa May walked into the room, there was this air of confidence,' she recalled. 'She has such a wonderfully positive attitude. The fact that she is a woman made no difference, as far as I was concerned.' It was that exact air that made the country breathe such a sigh of relief when she took over as Prime Minister and her appeal, such as it is and was, is not the same as that of Margaret Thatcher. Maggie, like it or not, had sex appeal and was not afraid to use it. Theresa didn't, and doesn't. Instead she exudes the air of a headmistress, kindly but slightly exasperated by her charges and disinclined to let them get away with anything.

Sonning didn't register on the national consciousness any more than Theresa herself did – the Clooney presence was still some way away – but for a woman who had been brought up in an Oxfordshire village, it must have felt like coming home. Three miles outside of Reading, it was once described by *Three Men in a Boat* author Jerome K. Jerome as 'the most fairy-like little nook on the whole river'. It has a pub, the Bull Inn, a riverside hotel, the Great House at Sonning, and even a little theatre, the Mill Theatre, which stands on Sonning

Eye, an island on the Thames. Local residents include Led Zeppelin guitarist Jimmy Page, illusionist Uri Geller and former England football manager Glenn Hoddle, while past residents include the playwright Sir Terence Rattigan and the English highwayman Dick Turpin. Nestled on the Thames, the village provides plenty of boating activity, while charming cottages rub shoulders with much larger mansions. An hour's drive from London, it was an idyllic spot.

Not that Theresa would have too much time to spend in her new home. On 2 May 1997, the country woke to discover that it had a Labour government for the first time in 18 years. There had been a massive 10.2 per cent swing to Labour from the Conservatives and the party now held 418 seats, the best result in its entire history; it had gained 145 seats, the Tories had lost 178. It was the Tories' worst showing since 1906, with no seats at all in Scotland and Wales, and high-profile names, including Michael Portillo, Malcolm Rifkind, Ian Lang, Michael Forsyth, Edwina Currie, Norman Lamont and David Mellor, all lost their seats. Indeed, Portillo looked so anguished when the result came in that a catchphrase, 'Were you up for Portillo?', did the rounds and although he did eventually find another seat and returned to the Commons, it is widely held that it was that night that destroyed the ambitions of a man once spoken of as a future prime minister. Of the sharp-suited, carefully coiffed new MP for Maidenhead, there was little interest outside her constituency. Certainly no one thought of her as a future PM.

The result did not put a stop to Tory infighting: quite the opposite, with various factions rounding on one another, all blaming each other for the severity of their defeat. John Major promptly resigned, saying, 'When the curtain falls, it is time to leave the stage,' and in time the undoubtedly impressive William Hague was elected as party leader, a poisoned chalice if ever there was one, and so it proved. But what has been all but forgotten is that in the course of that bitter leadership race, in which some MPs were made to look extremely foolish when it emerged that they had promised their vote to more than one of the five contenders and in at least one case to all five of them, Theresa maintained absolute silence on who she had backed. Even then she was to display a canny knack of maintaining her silence at crucial moments and managing to stay out of the divisive issues threatening to rend her party in two.

No one could have got the Tories into a reasonable state back then, such was the bile and recrimination spilling out from all sides, but William Hague, for all his unquestioned ability, was not the man to do the job. For a start, at thirty-six he was too young, and an attempt to capitalise on that by visiting a theme park wearing a baseball cap bearing the legend 'HAGUE' merely served to emphasise the fact that he looked as if he'd be a lot more comfortable in tweeds and a tie. He was also hampered by an appearance made when he was even younger, just sixteen, when he made a speech at the Conservatives Annual National Conference in 1977, telling delegates, 'half of you won't be here in thirty or forty years' time . . . but that others would have to live with consequences of a Labour government if it stayed in power.'

The delegates (including Margaret Thatcher) loved it, but that speech went on to haunt Hague throughout his career, as a teenage political nerd who spent his spare time reading Hansard. Even in later years he could never quite escape it, and for all the impressive work he did later, he could never really persuade the electorate he was a normal human being. There has always been a sense of early promise unfulfilled about William Hague and so what would have seemed to him to be a great opportunity back then turned out to be a huge misstep. Nor did it help that one of the Tory areas of conflict soon centred on the merits of getting rid of William Hague.

It was a baptism of fire for new MPs and it wasn't long before Theresa was getting a taste of life in the line of fire. She might have been new in the Commons, but there was a shortage of fresh talent in the latest intake and at any rate she was so fundamentally competent that her qualities soon began to shine through. In 1998 Hague appointed her as shadow spokesman for schools, disabled people and women, putting her up against the Labour education crew, at that stage headed by David Blunkett. The Conservative Shadow Minister was David Willetts and also on the team was Theresa's old friend, Damian Green. Theresa had worked on education on Merton Council, of course, which gave her an edge.

In truth, there was a slightly unpleasant undercut to some of the coverage she initially received in the national press. It was noted that she was not one of the new intake from think tanks, policy units or the ranks of special advisers but from the exceedingly less glamorous background of local government in south London. Of course this is now seen as a plus in her favour, but it wasn't always back then. There had been some sneering in gossip columns about the banal press releases she had put out in the run-up to the election, with one paper commenting, 'they make the Smurfs look like Pushkin'. Theresa ignored them all, as well she might.

About a week after her appointment, Theresa gave an interview to *The Guardian*, which was never going to be sympathetic to a Tory, but she did manage to give an early flavour of what she was thinking. On the thorny subject of women's issues, she commented, 'I think there are issues which affect women more than men. But it's a mistake to say, for example, childcare is just a woman's issue: parents should work together.' On being Conservative: 'I wasn't an unthinking Tory. I was on the right because of individual freedom. I suppose standing on your own two feet was part of my father's ethos of public service.'

And on Labour's education policy: 'We see in general terms a very bossy government, not just telling people they can't eat beef on the bone, but also in education, increasingly taking powers to the centre, and on the social policy side, where there is, I think, a concerning element of coercion.'

Labour's instinct to stick its nose into every conceivable area of life was becoming increasingly obvious at this stage and Theresa's instinct to keep the state out of personal concerns was equally coming through. She got another opportunity to tell Labour to stay out of it just a few days later when the Deputy Prime Minister, John Prescott, said that parents should stop driving their children to school and get them to cycle instead: 'It's mainly mums who drive their children to school and this is an attack on those women,' she said. 'Paramount in a parent's mind is safety and that is why most take their children to school in a car.' It was quite small beer compared to what was to come, but Theresa was showing herself not averse to a scrap, nor was she afraid to take on the big beasts of the day.

That she was making an impression was borne out by the fact that in July 1998, with concerns mounting over William Hague's performance as Tory leader, Theresa was for the first time spoken of as a potential party leader. It was quite a suggestion – she'd been in the Commons for only eighteen months, but hailing her as 'Maggie May', the *Mail on Sunday* suggested that she was a 'secret weapon', should Hague fall under the wheels of a Reliant Robin. Other names in the frame included Francis Maude, Liam Fox and the hapless Iain Duncan Smith, but the truth was that anyone with longer-term ambitions one day to enter Number 10 was well advised not to touch the Tory leadership with a bargepole. Infighting in the party was as strong as ever; compared to Labour, then still a well-oiled election fighting machine; they looked like amateurs, and amateurs riven with a loathing for one another, at that.

At any rate, no one outside the party had heard of Theresa May. She continued to work hard in the background, increasingly championing women's issues: she spoke out against forced marriage, taking officials in Islamabad and New Delhi to task for an obstructive attitude towards the problem of young British girls of Asian origin being married off to strangers, who were then allowed to come to the UK. Theresa was always vehemently opposed to positive discrimination in anything gender-related and it was understandable that she didn't want to be too closely associated with women's issues alone, as that could have led her into a political specialist interest area that would rule out her taking on a wider role.

But she appeared to be relaxing somewhat, able to see that some gender-related causes were not political suicide and emboldened, was also showing that she wasn't afraid to take on the status quo. There was another row with David Blunkett when he suggested imposing a timetable that parents would have to sign to guarantee their children were doing set amounts of homework (an obsession with imposing rules had 'gone over the top').

In January 1999, with no one but the party faithful taking much interest in what was going on within the Tory ranks, William Hague prepared for a reshuffle, which was widely considered to be a chance for him to break from the past, impose his own vision on the party and, crucially, attempt to make the Tories appear a little more woman-friendly than they were coming across. Labour was still in its honeymoon period, with Tony Blair fêted wherever he went, whereas the Tories were managing to come across as more out of touch than ever, especially where women were concerned. That same month Tory frontbencher Nick Gibb called Paymaster General Dawn Primarolo a 'stupid woman' on the floor of the House, prompting uproar and a reprimand from the Speaker, Betty Boothroyd, who forced him to withdraw his remark and apologise.

'You have insulted half the population with your remark about stupid women. I would like an apology as I happen to be one of them,' she snapped.

It was patently obvious that Theresa would be one of those promoted to increase the female-friendly aura Hague so desperately wanted to envelop the party with and with European elections looming in June, there was no time to be lost. At that point, just about the only high-profile woman of any stature in the party was Ann Widdecombe, the health spokesperson, and a very popular one at that. She spoke her mind, she patently cared about her constituents, she wasn't venal and she had a high moral ethos that she adhered to. But one high-profile woman was not enough. Apart from Theresa, other women who were being speculated about were Jacqui Lait, Caroline Spelman and Eleanor Laing, but all of them still prompted the same response from the electorate. And that response was: 'Who?'

It was a time of firsts as Theresa settled into her new role. In 1999 she made her first declaration in the Register of Members' Financial Interests and very modest it was too: she listed occasional broadcasting fees, honorary life membership for herself and Philip of the Maidenhead Conservative Club (the least they could do, one might have thought, for their sitting MP), a couple of dinners where they were guests of ARCO Chemical Europe and Southern Electric and some shareholdings in Prudential Corporation. There was no mention of entertaining on yachts, flights on private jets or lavish parties in the Seychelles. It was already very clear that was not Theresa's style. On a lighter note, it emerged that there was another Teresa May – without an 'h', except this one was a porn star. Theresa with an 'h' has always made light of it, although after she was elected prime minister, her namesake appeared in the headlines once more.

In due course Theresa was indeed made Shadow Education Secretary, as William Hague cleared out the old guard and appointed the new, although the average voter would have been hard placed to put a face to the name. The other women promoted at the time were Ann Widdecombe, who became Shadow Home Secretary, and Angela Browning as Shadow Trade and Industry Secretary, although among those in the know, Theresa's elevation was the most significant move because it was by far the biggest promotion, an indicator that she was destined for greater things (something Hague was not slow to point out that he had recognised early on through that appointment, years later when he himself had left the political stage). The shadow chancellor, arguably the most important role after Hague himself, was Francis Maude, later elevated to the House of Lords after a long and successful political career.

But one of the few advantages of being in a party so very much reduced in size was that, for the able, the opportunities were there and for all that the Tories wanted a few more women in the limelight, they were only prepared to promote them if they could actually do the job. The fact that Theresa became a shadow minister so quickly was in part due to the fact that the talent pool was depleted, but it was also because she had very speedily shown that she was actually able to do the job. It meant she had been thrown in at the deep end and so had to learn fast; over on Labour, paradoxically, because there were so many MPs and so many of them were women, there was none of the same impetus to learn how to get on with doing the job.

Theresa, as was to be expected, proved solidly able in the job. She attacked the government over a shortage of homegrown teachers when it turned out people were being imported from Australia and the United States to fill the gaps; she followed that up with further condemnation when it emerged that one school in South Marston, a village close to Swindon, was so short of space that it had to hold classes in a tent; she had another pop at David Blunkett over excessive interference in schools' homework policies and she criticised further powers being handed to Ofsted, the education watchdog.

This was followed up by an attack on the government for failing to reduce the bureaucracy surrounding schools and a highly critical take on a BBC series teaching children about sex (one particular bone of contention came when teenage girls were told 'casual sex is fine, if you can handle it'). At the Conservative Party Conference in October 1999 Theresa won a standing ovation when she made her first speech from the platform, promising a 'bonfire of controls' in education – 'We believe that heads, teachers and governors know what is best for their pupils and their schools, that local needs are best addressed by local decisions,' she declared, but while the Tory faithful loved it, the rest of the country, still in thrall to their Bambi prime minister, couldn't have cared less what the Conservatives had to say.

The one and only thing that even slightly engaged the interest of the wider public was that Michael Portillo was rumoured to be heading back to the Commons via the desirable seat of Kensington and Chelsea, which had recently come up for grabs following the death of the incumbent MP Alan Clark in September 1999. This was considered to have major implications for William Hague's leadership, not least because it was widely believed that had Portillo not lost his seat in the 1997 election, he would be at the head of his party now. In the event Portillo did get in, although right from the start it was obvious that he was a changed man.

Still the urge continued to try and seize the initiative back from Labour. There was some controversy when Theresa proposed schools league tables for seven-year-olds, which was widely criticised by the teaching unions and totally ignored elsewhere. She retaliated by fiercely attacking Islington Council's proposal to pay children £3.50 an hour to do their homework and led a chorus of indignation when it was suggested that students from EU countries might be able to avoid university tuition fees while British students were forced to pay.

Theresa was actually highlighting some very real problems that were to mushroom over the years, not least when proposals were put forward in 2000 designed to usher non-academic pupils into taking degrees. Sixteen years after the fact we have universities not worthy of the name pushing students into dreadful levels of debt in the pursuit of worthless degrees, but while Theresa quite clearly highlighted the dangers of this happening, no one paid any attention, not down to any lacking on her part but because the Conservative Party continued to be seen as utterly irrelevant. While these worthy pursuances of her job were reported on in the serious press, the headlines centred on Tory backstabbing and disloyalty: the Hague and Portillo Show. She also made some very salient points about Labour's ongoing quest to close down the country's remaining grammar schools (again a topic she tackled almost immediately on becoming Prime Minister), attacking David Blunkett repeatedly on the subject, and congratulating the House of Lords on overturning legislation that would have threatened their future. For all the fact that she was making little impact on the wider populace it was becoming increasingly clear to her colleagues that Theresa May had certainly mastered her brief.

And apart from her continuing ability to hold Labour to account, Theresa was proving herself to be a good and hard-working constituency MP, increasingly popular with the people of Sonning and carving out a good reputation in everything she did. It is never very rewarding being in opposition, especially when your party is quite as unpopular as the Tories were at that stage, while the Prime Minister in power was still unaccountably one of the most popular politicians in living memory. And although it was certainly a time to listen and learn, there was worse – much worse – to come.

9

THE QUIET MAN

L ooking back on the history of the Conservatives in the early years of the twenty-first century, it is as if a collective madness swept the party. Having elected one unphotogenic candidate who was unable to connect with the majority of voters in the country, the Tories now found themselves on a course to elect a similar second candidate also unable to connect with the majority of voters in the country and this at a time when the country had never needed an effective opposition more. Bambi was proving to be a less 'straight sort of guy' than he had previously been given credit for, with unexpected warmongering tendencies which were to be violently and catastrophically unleashed in the wake of the world's worst terrorist atrocity, with all the tragedy that was to unfurl. But rather than fight the incumbents, Her Majesty's loyal opposition was still intent on knocking one another into the further reaches of Kingdom Come, something that showed no signs of abating as the new century began. Matricide had unhinged the brain.

After Michael Portillo had returned to the Commons in 2000, William Hague sought to neutralise the threat by making him Shadow Chancellor, a generous gesture designed to prove that he believed they could work together and that he welcomed Portillo's presence. Unfortunately it didn't work. Supporters of the two men continued to tear chunks out of each other, while Hague himself continued to be the object of some suspicion. He couldn't win: a claim to have drunk '14 pints a day' as a teenager incurred derision, his reference to Britain as a 'foreign land' due to increased immigration had Michael Heseltine, no stranger to disloyalty to a party leader, openly confiding he was uncertain whether he could support a Tory Party led by Hague and despite repeatedly and comprehensively trouncing Blair in Prime Minister's Questions, his success inside the House could not translate into votes outside it. Hague bravely and confidently continued to insist that the Tories could win the 2001 election, but wiser beings knew they didn't stand a chance. The party was widely perceived to have shifted to the right, remained sharply divided over the EU and there was now the issue of whether to adopt the euro to contend with.

On Thursday, 7 June 2001, Britain went to the polls and returned a Labour government. The Tories increased their number of MPs to the tune of one, the Liberal Democrats under the late Charles Kennedy gained a reasonably respectable 52, while Labour held on to its gigantic majority, losing only 5 seats and ending up with 413 MPs. It was pretty much a repeat of 1997, the only real difference being that voter turnout was sharply down at just 59.4 per cent. Some voters might have been getting disillusioned with Labour but they were in no mood to turn to the Conservatives. William Hague duly resigned.

While she had been working steadily on her brief, Theresa did not have a high-profile role in the campaign, leading to sniping that Hague had enlisted very few women in senior positions, but given the mess the party was in, as far as she was concerned it was probably just as well. The high-profile brigade lined up for a fight for the leadership: Michael Portillo launched his campaign with a vow to scrap the controversial Section 28 legislation outlawing the promotion of homosexuality. Theresa was an early supporter, alongside Archie Norman and Tim Yeo. The other contenders were Iain Duncan Smith, Kenneth Clarke, David Davis and Michael Ancram; Ann Widdecombe, despite her undoubted popularity among the party faithful, decided not to run.

At the outset it looked to be a shoo-in for the leader-in-waiting, Michael Portillo, whose failure to challenge John Major for the leadership in 1995 continued to haunt him, but who looked to be at last stepping up to the challenge. Suave, debonair and good-looking, Portillo appeared to be the modernising figure that the party was looking for and this can only be the reason why he decided now was the time to go public about the homosexual experiences of his youth. Just a few years later this wouldn't cause a ripple, but at the time it caused a sensation: the rumours had been doing the rounds for years, but the safest and most sensible strategy at that stage would have been to rise above them rather than confirm everything.

The shock caused to the party was palpable and matters were not helped when more information came to light about his behaviour during the 1995 leadership election, when it appeared that he was backing John Major on the one hand and having banks of telephones installed in a makeshift HQ to mount a challenge on the other. Later on it was remarked that Portillo imploded during that period and although he was to stay on until the next election, this was clearly the moment when he started to lose interest in a political career. Portillo had started out as a hardline right-winger who once made a notorious speech at a Party Conference extolling the virtues of the SAS; now he seemed to have made some sort of journey to the opposite side of the party with the result that no one really knew what he stood for. He was about to join Michael Heseltine and countless others in the category of crown prince, who never actually ascended the throne.

The rounds of voting began. Michael Ancram was the first to drop out, followed by David Davis, and then, shocking to some, Michael Portillo. It later emerged that tactical voting had done for him. Some bits of the party were 'not quite sure whether they were more Europhobic than homophobic, or more homophobic than Europhobic,' said Kenneth Clark. 'They were the hardcore who are normally found on the hard right, which had been Michael Portillo's natural constituency until two or three years ago.'

The two remaining candidates, Kenneth Clarke and Iain Duncan Smith, took it out to the party membership and spent three bruising months slugging it out, but the Europhobes were to do for Ken, too, as he was just too pro-EU for their taste. The election result was expected to be announced on 11 September 2001. That date, of course, was the date of the terrible attacks in the United States, killing 2,996 people, with two hijacked planes flying into the Twin Towers, another into the Pentagon and a fourth brought down by brave passengers in a field in Pennsylvania. They knew they were doomed but they were determined the terrorists would not prevail.

The world lost its innocence that day; indeed the state of profound shock that attack elicited still resonates today. But for the purposes of this narrative it is best to move away and to observe simply that the Tory's election result was delayed for two days, when it was announced that Iain Duncan Smith, or 'IDS' as he was popularly known, was to be the next Tory Party leader. He was given a cautious – very cautious – welcome, leading one right-leaning newspaper to observe 'We like the cut of his jib.'

IDS had his own history with the party: Norman Tebbit's

successor in the constituency of Chingford, he had constantly needled John Major when that hapless individual was running the show, above all on the subject of Maastricht. This was not necessarily a bad thing in the eyes of at least some of the Tories in Parliament, nor indeed in the eyes of some ex-Tory leaders, when Margaret Thatcher came out in his support. In the end the contest yet again was down to the EU: Ken Clarke, who would almost certainly have steered the Tories back on track much faster, was denied the leadership because he was a Europhile; IDS got the prize *because* he was a Europhobe. His tenure as party leader was to prove an utter disaster, although at least his dire performance would act to bring the Conservatives back to their senses. This just could not go on.

But it did. IDS reshuffled his Shadow Cabinet, with half of William Hague's Cabinet either stepping down or being sacked, and in the process Theresa got transport, local government and the regions. And it took no time for the criticisms to start flooding in: the new crowd was too inexperienced, too right wing, too Eurosceptic... The new crowd was dominated by Michael Howard, Oliver Letwin, John Whittingdale and David Davis, while Theresa was singled out by one journalist as one of three Shadow Cabinet members who were 'hardly going to set the television screens, or the floor of the House of Commons, alight'. As a matter of fact, she was wrong there: Theresa might have been part of a political grouping at that point going nowhere, but the time was now fast approaching when she was going to leap from the shadows into the political limelight. There were further signs too that she was taking up the cause of helping women in politics: while still fiercely opposed to all-female shortlists, she co-authored a paper calling for 50–50 male/female lists in marginal Tory seats.

It quickly emerged that IDS was not just going to be out of touch with the electorate, but with his own party, too. From the outset it was made clear to him that senior party figures would be keeping an eye on him to make sure he didn't drag the party too far to the right; meanwhile allies of Kenneth Clarke and Michael Portillo lost no time in voicing their disquiet. There was no cheer in that year's Party Conference, which on the first day saw a warning from the Centre for Policy Studies – a right-wing think tank – that if they didn't regain the centre ground then they would face electoral oblivion. At times that was beginning to appear a real possibility.

Theresa kept her head down and ploughed on but there were increasing signs that she was turning her attention to the problem of attracting more women into politics and she was also among the many who were appalled when it emerged that Jo Moore, a special adviser to the Transport Secretary Stephen Byers, had suggested in an email that was subsequently leaked that September 11 was a 'good day to bury bad news'. It was 'heartless' and 'disgracefully cynical,' she said and the row did in fact claim Moore's scalp. But behind the scenes the Labour Leader was beginning to plan a very different response to September 11, one that would lead to global disaster but one the Conservatives were in no position to sense or counter at the time, given that the party remained on its knees.

Theresa became embroiled in the row, repeatedly calling for Jo Moore to go because she was shadowing Moore's boss at Transport and with her usual efficiency, mastered the brief and sought to keep Labour on their toes, not least by bringing pressure to bear on Byers over a highly controversial decision to put the privatised railway infrastructure company Railtrack into administration, a decision that was taken over the weekend, ignored the regulator, Tom Winsor, and had the effect of renationalising the UK's railway infrastructure through the creation of Network Rail. It was a real scandal and contributed to Byers' own return to the back benches.

There was some evidence that money had been withheld from Railtrack that could have saved it and Theresa went on the attack, but the fact is that the party itself was in such a weak position, neither she nor anyone else could do any proper damage. An examination of the Labour years, which is not the remit here, shows over and again appalling policy errors, misjudgements, flawed thinking and the secretive implementation of courses of action that were never run past the population, such as the encouragement of widespread immigration into the UK, that should have been picked up and fought by the Tories, but they were in no position to do so. As long as the vicious Tory infighting continued, they would never be an effective electoral force.

At least it was giving Theresa the experience of differing areas of government as well as allowing her to prove her own worth. Meanwhile Stephen Byers was proving to be a hapless Transport Secretary and not just as far as Railtrack was concerned: as 2002 began, the rail services were in a terrible mess, with thousands of passengers stranded by strikes. Blair called in the former BBC Director General Lord (John) Birt to sort out the mess – 'This looks like the final nail in Stephen Byers's coffin. His job has been effectively handed over to one of Tony's cronies but I doubt that the country's appalling transport problems will be solved by a man whose idea of a traffic hold-up is his chauffeur turning up five minutes late,' snapped Theresa – and this could have gone on for years, when circumstances conspired to give her an opportunity that would finally propel her into the public eye. While many blamed Byers for the country's transport mess, and after several months of sustained attack from Theresa he finally left his post, just about no one outside those who were interested in politics gave Theresa any credit for trying to hold him to account for the simple reason that they didn't have the faintest idea who she was.

That was about to change.

The chairman of the Conservative Party at that point was David Davis, one of the original leadership contenders, but there were complaints that exhausted, perhaps, by the infighting and the dire state of the party, he had shown little appetite for the job. The grass roots membership in particular was alleged to feel he was ignoring them, although it should be said that Tory infighting was so vicious at this point that the reality is that this was also the result of stirring and machinations from various party factions. Another problem was that Davis very much represented the old guard, while anyone with a vision could see that the party needed to modernise and find itself more in step with the times. He was also, more to the point, accused of plotting against IDS, and it was felt in some quarters that IDS was concerned about being overshadowed. At any rate, in yet another attempt to modernise the Tories, stamp his authority on the party and so forth, IDS decided to sack Davis, who was informed of the decision when he was on leave in Florida, and replace him with someone else – but who?

IDS had already shown a desire to promote the interests of women in the party by refusing to join the Carlton Club, a Conservative club which at that time offered full membership only to men and traditionally always had the Leader of the Tories as a member – Mrs Thatcher had been made an honorary member of the establishment. Now he decided to go one step further and appoint a woman for the first time ever as chairman of the Tories, with the names in the frame being Caroline Spelman, the Shadow International Development Secretary, and favourite for the role, Gillian Shephard, former Education Secretary, or one Theresa May.

In the event, of course, the job went to Theresa, with a raft of other top jobs reshuffled at the same time – Davis ended up in charge of local government, shadowing the Labour deputy leader, the buffoonish John Prescott, although IDS strongly denied that he'd been demoted or sacked. It was said in later years that Theresa lamented not being the first ever British female prime minister, but she did make it to become the first ever female Tory party chairman and it is clear that although the hapless IDS was not the man to do it, it was at that stage that the Tories showed the first signs of once more becoming a fighting force. They were still at one another's throats and would remain so for some time; also there were still very few female MPs and so this represented, among much else, a desire to signal to the wider electorate that the Conservatives were the party for everyone. Theresa said she was 'absolutely delighted' as well she might, adding that the party was changing and 'open, decent and tolerant . . . committed to reforming public services'.

Although Theresa's appointment of course made waves, as the first female incumbent of the post, the real attention remained on Tory infighting, with inevitable comparisons to rearranging the deckchairs on RMS *Titanic*. This did nothing to stop the anguish in the party or to heal any wounds. IDS had got rid of a trouble-making rival was the gist of a lot of the coverage and there were also jibes about tokenism – in other words, completely underestimating both the significance of the appointment and Theresa's own formidable intelligence and ability. By this time it was becoming increasingly apparent that IDS was nowhere near up to the job of running the party

– the *Daily Express*'s Patrick O'Flynn compared him to Frank Spencer of the BBC sitcom *Some Mothers Do 'Ave 'Em* – while elsewhere it was written: 'One little-known figure, David Davis, was yesterday replaced by another, Theresa May.'

In some quarters David Davis was written off and while he went on to hold senior positions in the Shadow Cabinet, he was not given a senior government post – until Theresa became Prime Minister and made him Secretary of State for exiting the European Union, a considerably more nuanced appointment than she was given credit for at the time. But the bitterness engendered by Davis's demotion at the time only intensified, with IDS putting him in charge of the party for a week while he, IDS, went on holiday, as a sort of consolation prize and to show there was no bad feeling.

No one was fooled.

Because Theresa was such an unknown to all but a small circle of people the odd profile began to appear, emphasising the solid City background, the modest background, the stable marriage and the odd sketch writer also mentioned the nifty-looking shoes the new party chairman (Theresa made it clear she did not wish to be called 'chairwoman' or 'chairperson') liked to wear. In fact, there was quite a bit of mention about her appearance, with references to lilac leather jackets and black leather trousers, but still the public refused to sit up and take notice. Neither did Labour, still very much in the ascendant and blithely unconcerned about Tory woes.

A small amount of public recognition began to come her

way, as evidenced by an interview Theresa gave to the *Sunday Telegraph* in July 2002: 'The first time somebody recognises you in the street, you think "Ooh, gosh!" But as it happens more and more, you just long for the moment when . . . I mean, it's not like being Kylie Minogue and being recognised everywhere. But sometimes you wish you could get round Waitrose without somebody coming up and raising an issue.' But that recognition came as much on the back of the Railtrack row as it did on becoming party chairman, and Theresa realised that she was going to come under a lot more scrutiny in her new role. In that interview she rebuffed questions about childlessness, talked the talk about modernising the party, the need for party unity (some hope!) and came across as very good-humoured. But there was nothing about radical reform or the ambitions to get to the very top.

In July 2002 the Tories' attempts to make themselves into something that resembled, ever so slightly, the rest of the population continued when Alan Duncan became the first Conservative MP to openly declare that he was gay. It is a mark of how different the times were back then that IDS immediately wrote to him to reassure him that it would not affect his career. Theresa may have been a vicar's daughter, but she was progressive in her views about gay rights and promptly announced that this was a sign the Tories were 'an open, decent and tolerant' party. Not everyone agreed and some high-profile Tories spoke out about washing dirty linen in public but it was indeed a sign that times were changing and also a sign that Theresa, as much as anyone else, knew they had to.

As IDS announced that he was launching 'Phase Two' of his leadership to put an end to recent tensions – some hope – senior party members, Theresa among them, began the painful process of self-examination to see just how they were going to get themselves out of the mess they were in. The Party Conference was approaching and this was a time to review recent events and chart the path ahead. No one paid much attention to another piece of news that came out around that time, namely that donations to the Labour Party were plunging, a very early sign of public disillusion, but it was to be years before that trend actually translated into votes. Meanwhile the Tories continued in their disarray: matters were not helped when the veteran politician Lord (Norman) Tebbit called for the 'squabbling children' of Conservative Central Office to go, referring to chief executive Mark MacGregor and strategy director Dominic Cummings specifically, and prompting a reply from the former party chairman Francis Maude, who said that voters wanted 'thoughtful, intelligent people who seem to be living on the same planet'.

While they might have done, they weren't going to get it. The Tories looked like a 'poor man's version of the Church of England on a bad day,' pronounced senior Tory Sir Nicholas Soames. 'Do we look like a serious, sane, responsible political party ready to take power? No.' IDS was being undermined by 'spotty youths, researchers, assistants and party apparatchiks,' said Lord Tebbit. There were calls for IDS to go: 'He has actually been leader for less than a year now. It is only eleven months or so since he became leader,' said Francis Maude. 'It is not going to be an overnight turn-around. These things don't happen like that. What there is going to be is a steady pull-back, a steady winning back of people's respect, which we are not going to do by launching into all-out bare-knuckle fights with Labour about everything.'

The trouble was they were launching into all-out bare-knuckle fights with each other. Then there were rumours that supporters of Michael Portillo were planning a break-away 'Start Again Party': 'That is a lot of silliness and a bit of misinterpretation, as far as I can understand it, by people who are on the fringes and I don't think that is of any account at all,' said Francis Maude. And so it went on: what was needed now was a headmistress figure to read them the riot act – and that is what they got.

Any female politician knows that she will be judged on her appearance – rightly or wrongly, it's inevitable – and Theresa May certainly dressed rather more nattily than many another female MP. At that unenlightened stage in the British psyche, any politician wearing leather caused palpitations and she did so regularly, but to call Theresa a style icon, either then or now, is nonsense. She might have claimed a 'passion for fashion' but she got it wrong quite as much as she got it right and frequently wore clothes that really didn't suit her (something that continues to this day). A much better example of a politician dressing for high office is Margaret Thatcher, who adopted a near uniform of smart Aquascutum suit, pelmet hairdo and good jewellery. But Theresa still knew that what she wore would attract attention and she also knew that if she were to have any hope of making it to the top of politics, people would need to know who she was. And so she delved into her wardrobe, produced a pair of kitten heels and prepared to make real headlines – and she did.

10

THE NASTY
PARTY

October 2002 and the party faithful had gathered in Bournemouth, and a very miserable time it was to be a Tory, too. There was yet more uproar about yet more unsavoury revelations because, carefully timed to tie in with the annual Conservative Party Conference, a new book had been published. Edwina Currie's *Diaries 1987–1992* had just come out and in them the former MP, who had always maintained an extremely high profile, had made the extraordinary revelation that she and the former Prime Minister John Major had carried on an affair for four years, from 1984 to 1988, when they were both married to other people.

Until then Major had seemed very much the grey man of British politics, the most exciting revelation about him prior to this being that his wife liked to freeze left-over cheese, but this cast him in a new light altogether. It made a mockery – if further mockery were needed to be made – of his 'Back to Basics' campaign, cast fresh light on his very dubious judgement and produced the last thing the party needed, a fresh batch of headlines shrieking about 'Tory sleaze'. Interviewed on the eve of the conference, Theresa was asked for her take: 'I was surprised,' she told the *Daily Telegraph* in 2002. 'Then I thought – let's face it: it happened fourteen years ago. It's a personal matter for the two individuals involved. I don't think it's damaging – it's not about today's Conservative Party. Today's Conservative Party has moved on.'

The Telegraph (like every other paper in the country) promptly embarked on a list of horrors that sometimes seemed to dominate every news item on TV during that febrile era in Tory Party history: former grandee Jeffrey Archer was in prison serving a sentence for perjury but had been caught at a party given by Gillian Shephard MP, contravening prison rules and attracting a good deal of negative publicity, unhelpfully reminding the public of one of the more colourful Conservatives the leading lights were now thoroughly embarrassed about. Jonathan Aitken, meanwhile, another Tory who had served a prison sentence for perjury following stories about his business dealings with Saudi Arabia, was now out of the clink but still making the headlines regularly as he sought to make public his shame and to carve out a new life for himself. Neil and Christine Hamilton, meanwhile, who had been named in the Cash for

Questions scandal a few years earlier, were yet again back in the news for reasons for which they were entirely blameless but which were nonetheless bizarre: they had been accused of sexually assaulting trainee lecturer Nadine Milroy-Sloan, a crime of which they were completely innocent but which nonetheless, inevitably, hit the headlines. The woman involved was a fantasist and accused of perverting the course of justice, but it was yet more negative publicity and sleazy at that – hardly the kind of thing that party leaders wanted plastered all over the newspapers as they sought to rebuild the Tories' shattered fortunes. The grassroots were torn between horror and disgust: how could a once-great political machine have come to this?

Theresa, inevitably, was questioned about all these ongoing nightmares and was cautious in her reply: 'I think, frankly, that although these people were prominent in the party in the past, it's not something that impinges on people's perception of the Conservatives today. The party is changing. We have to make clear that we're not constantly looking back to the past, that we're interested in the problems people face today and will face in the future – a party that's looking forward and moving on.'

Still, it would have been enough to try the patience of a saint. This was Theresa's first Party Conference as its chairman, the news had been unremittingly bad since she'd taken over and looked to get no better: it almost seemed as if fate was conspiring to bring one sleaze-laden incident after another to the fore. And so when she slipped on a dark purple suit (one of her better wardrobe choices) and a pair of snazzy heels, she might have been forgiven for being in a bad mood. Quite how bad was about to become clear.

The delegates wanted their new chairman to make her mark and they got it . . . in spades. Some Conservatives behaved 'disgracefully' in the past, she said (no prizes for guessing who she was thinking of) and that it was time the party faced up to the 'uncomfortable truth' that it was sometimes perceived as the 'nasty party': 'In recent years a number of politicians have behaved disgracefully and then compounded their offences by trying to evade responsibility. We all know who they are. Let's face it, some of them have stood on this platform . . .' She was pulling no punches. The impression of sleaze had been 'reinforced by what we have read in the newspapers over the last two weeks.' Delegates' jaws dropped as she went on: the public had become cynical about 'spinning and counter spinning . . . Politicians need to look at themselves. And that, ladies and gentlemen, includes Conservatives.'

And then came applause. Theresa then laid into 'mindless partisanship that passes for debate' in modern politics: 'Some Tories have tried to make political capital by demonising minorities instead of showing confidence in all the citizens of our country. Some Tories have indulged themselves in petty feuding or personal sniping instead of getting behind a leader who is doing an enormous amount to change a party which has suffered two massive landslide defeats.' They needed to change 'behaviour and attitudes' to alter the public perception of 'the nasty party': 'No more glib moralising. No more hypocritical finger wagging.'

There was more, but she had entirely made her point.

The speech caused a sensation. Theresa had been extremely brave: she had not ignored the zooful of elephants in the room as she must have been tempted to and tackled the issues head on. It was 'a stiletto in the Tories' heart,' opined the *Daily Telegraph*, and was followed up by Oliver Letwin's denunciation of the party's 'weird' reliance on white male MPs (something that has all but been forgotten, given how much it was overshadowed by Theresa's speech). But not everyone was thrilled. That phrase 'nasty party' hit home and to this day there are those who maintain Theresa shouldn't have said it. She was handing a gift to the Conservatives' enemies, they warned, for if such a senior member of the Conservative Party took such a dim view of her own party, how must it look to everyone else? In reality, of course, this was the real moment the Tories began to modernise but such was the hysteria surrounding them that no one really understood the full significance of such a speech.

Iain Duncan Smith made a memorable speech that year too, one that blew up in his face almost as soon as he said it. He had, alas, been shown to be lacking in any form of charisma and attempted to turn this to his advantage: 'Do not underestimate the determination of a quiet man,' he said, which meant that for the next year practically every time he got up in the Commons to speak, Labour MPs would put their fingers to their lips and murmur 'Shush!' Another year of misery followed. Theresa proved herself more than up to her brief and after that combination of choice phraseology and kitten heels found that she had at last established herself firmly in the public eye but there was nothing the party could do to help itself (or if there was, it wasn't doing it). Over and again she was forced to defend not only her party, but her party leader too; it was a miserable time to be chairman of a party now more divided than it had ever been.

Rows were everywhere. John Bercow, who like Portillo seemed to have made the journey from extreme right of the party to very liberal left, called on the Tories (and thus Theresa) to bring in all-women shortlists, a step she continued to refuse to make, and he followed that up with an attack on IDS. Tim Yeo took a clear pop at Theresa's 'nasty party' speech when he accused some Tories of being stuck in guilt mode and even Theresa's own neck of the woods came under attack, when in a bizarre episode, Maidenhead, at the heart of her constituency, was described as an 'affluent riverside town with prosperous – if somewhat spoiled by the gin and Jag brigade – villages'. This was part of a Parliamentary answer from Pensions Secretary Andrew Smith and a livid Theresa demanded an apology; meanwhile the newspapers sent reporters to the two constituencies to count the number of Jaguars they could find and question the locals on their gin consumption.

Matters were descending into farce.

Iain Duncan Smith kept giving speeches in which he asserted that the Tories were on their way back to power. But no one listened and no one believed him and stories continued to circulate about plotters assembling to rid the party of their lame duck leader. Duncan Smith didn't help matters by employing an occupational psychologist, Professor Jo Silvester, to try to enlist more 'sympathetic' and 'representative'(for which read 'female') candidates for the party, which of course handed the headline writers the opportunity to crow that the Tories needed a shrink.

Above all else the problem of trying to attract more female candidates would not go away, so much so that in January 2003, the party halted its selection process for candidates for the next General Election amid concerns over the lack of women, although this was presented as being a way to concentrate on the forthcoming local elections in May. Theresa, who can lay claim to be a Tory moderniser from well before David Cameron got in on the act, was at the forefront of all this and it was she, more than anyone else, who was charged with making the change. This is tricky territory for a female politician: Margaret Thatcher avoided it altogether while Theresa was keen to make a difference, but not to the extent of positive discrimination. 'Many people in the party still have a stereotyped image of what an MP looks like, and it is a man, with a wife and two children,' she told *The Guardian*. 'I think too many people perhaps look at candidates on the basis of who are they going to enjoy having a drink with on a Sunday morning, rather than who is going to be able to deal with a constituent who comes into the surgery with a case of domestic violence. What is needed,' she added, 'is a proper job description for being an MP, setting out the professional skills needed to do the job.' Unfortunately, as she was seeking to promote the cause of women, elsewhere in the party the London Conservative Agents was preparing to hold its annual fundraising in a lap-dancing club.

Further furore surrounded an episode concerning Nikki Page, an ex-model who wanted to run as London mayor, who was tacitly supported by IDS (and who ended up in a relationship with John Redwood). After she was turfed out of the race early on, Theresa flatly refused requests to reinstall her, making the point that she was her own woman, but creating a great deal of tension with her party leader. It was ironic, given how desperate the Tories were to find more women candidates, but this woman was clearly deemed unsuitable for the role.

Meanwhile other problems that affected the entire country were simmering away in the background. Blair and the US President George Bush were clearly making plans to attack Iraq and both IDS and Theresa were supportive. Concerns about immigration – or more specifically at that point, asylum seekers who might not have been all they seemed – were growing, but the 'straight sort of ' – which for the media and public had morphed into 'straight kinda guy' – and his cohorts had very successfully managed to steer the debate in such a way that any politician who said anything about it was immediately branded a racist. It was a deliberate trap that had been set for the Tories and for a time it worked: while many clearly wanted to make the point that a huge problem was getting a lot worse, and in doing so creating a culture in which politicians were entirely losing touch with most people in the country, who were starting to feel increasingly disenfranchised, every time anyone said anything, they were labelled a bigot. It was utter cynicism on the part of the Labour Party, created entirely for short-term gain and with cavalier disregard for either the future of the country or the wishes of the people they represented. It was also to lead directly to the referendum vote of 2016 that would see Britain choose to leave the EU.

There was further chaos when IDS sacked two Tory modernisers, Mark MacGregor, chief executive of the party, and Rick Nye without consulting the party board (or Theresa), replacing them with Barry Legg, a move that triggered another attack from Michael Portillo and speculation that Theresa herself would be next in the firing line – a previous Portillo supporter, she was still being lumped in that camp. Amid rumours that he was going to replace her with John Redwood, IDS was forced to issue a denial that her job was at risk and given that she'd been in it for barely more than six months at this stage, such speculation was a mark of quite the extent of the party's appalling inner turmoil.

There was talk that the modernising project hadn't worked and that there would be a return to 'traditional' Conservative values, interpreted by most people as a lurch to the right. A full civil war was now being waged, with IDS and the hardliners on one side and Michael Portillo's modernisers on the other. Portillo himself might have been on his way out of politics but he was having one final blast while he was still there. 'I can't figure out what is going on at [Conservative] Central Office, I would be very pleased if anyone could tell me,' he told BBC News. 'All I have seen really over the last few days is what appear to be self-inflicted wounds and our party plunged back into crisis, and I'm sorry about that.'

Theresa was forced into the role of peacemaker, holding soothing talks with both representatives of the grassroots and indeed Tory grandees, all of whom were furious that they weren't being listened to and fearful with every further back that was stabbed, that the Tories would never see power again. There were assertions from some quite senior political observers that the Conservatives were finished as a political party and certainly, while all this infighting was going on, there was no hope of reclaiming past glories. Theresa was forced on the defensive and a glimpse of her inner steel was revealed for the first time to the public: 'With due respect to Michael Portillo – and indeed to John Redwood – neither of them is leader or chairman of this party,' she said. 'I am the chairman of the party and I am remaining chairman of the party.'

Anyone who thought that Theresa, with her kitten heels

and somewhat eccentric wardrobe, was a pushover was in for a second thought, it seemed.

Meanwhile Portillo upped the offensive against IDS, accusing him of putting Theresa in an impossible position and 'violating' the party. 'Her position appears to be impossible,' he told Radio 4's *The World at One*. 'She's been briefed against, changes have been made to the party that she should have been consulted about. It looks very bad.' IDS was guilty of 'perplexing' behaviour by sacking MacGregor. He had traded the 'extraordinary talent' of Mr MacGregor for the former right-winger Legg. 'You don't look tall if you surround yourself by short grasses. You look tall if you surround yourself by the tallest grasses . . . To surround yourself with lesser people and with people who agree with you is not a sign of strength. What I see is a narrowing of the party and that I think is worrying and I think sad.'

It wasn't an intervention exactly aimed at calming the situation and indeed, it did not. Instead, in a situation that was compared the former Foreign Secretary's attack on Margaret Thatcher that resulted in the leadership challenge that forced her out, many felt that Portillo, albeit with no further leadership ambitions of his own, was preparing the ground for IDS to be shown the door and certainly rumours of a leadership challenge were circulating widely now. IDS responded by calling Portillo, 'Self-indulgent to the point of madness.' There was no chance of peace breaking out any time soon.

However, IDS did at least show some common sense when he appointed Theresa in July 2002 to a new committee created to reform Conservative Central Office (CCO), a move widely interpreted as an olive branch. She in turn called on the Tories to unite behind him. But hostilities still broke out at every turn: after the Tories snapped up more than 560 seats in the following May's local elections, the event was marred by the resignation of Crispin Blunt, who called IDS a 'handicap' who made no impact on the electorate and although seen as a failed coup attempt against the party leader, this tale of rivalry, suicidal stupidity, arrogance, vanity and hubris was finally nearing an end. This was followed by the resignation of Barry Legg but by this time, with the country nearing the outbreak of war and collapsing trust in the Labour Party – which did not fully show through at the polls – the public had more to worry about than a group of navel-gazing politicos who seemed bent on destroying their own party simply to exact some sort of petty revenge.

In the 2003 autumn conference IDS, in another attempt to assert his authority, informed delegates, 'The quiet man is turning up the volume.' A few weeks later he was deposed and in November 2003 replaced by Michael Howard, much to the enormous relief of just about everyone in the party: the Tories might still be unelectable but at least someone with leadership qualities was in charge. Howard moved Theresa from the chairmanship, giving the post to Liam Fox and

Lord Saatchi (two men doing the work of one woman), and made her Shadow Secretary of State for Transport instead. That year she also became a Privy Councillor, a member of the board that advises the Monarch. The following year she became Shadow Secretary of State for Culture, Media and Sport. Life in opposition can be pretty joyless, though, and so Theresa kept her head down, tended to her constituency, toured the country to try to encourage the party faithful and prepared for the next Tory election defeat.

By the time the next General Election was held in 2005, the public love affair with Labour was beginning to wane, although it was to falter on for a few more years. In 2003 Blair had finally made the momentous decision to send British troops to be part of the invasion of Iraq ('finally' being a moot word, with some people believing the decision had been taken quietly well before then), a highly controversial move from the outset, although at that point most people still believed that the Iraqi President Saddam Hussein possessed weapons of mass destruction that could be used in an attack on the West. Labour was also supported by the Tories in this decision.

The era of mass immigration had also begun in earnest now, another highly unpopular initiative that had never been run past the public, and the 'straight kinda guy' was having to deal with in-fighting inside his own party, not least frequent and violent assaults on his own position by his chancellor, Gordon Brown. Opinion polls were beginning to say that the public did not find the Prime Minister 'trustworthy' – indeed, he was placed at the bottom of one such list.

It was not quite the sunny uplands of yesteryear for Blair this time around, with electoral disillusionment growing, and it was his own good fortune that the Tories, while beginning to make themselves look slightly more competent than previously, were still nowhere near looking like a party fit for government. But under the stabilising influence of Michael Howard, the fightback proper had begun.

Under the slogan, 'Are you thinking what we're thinking? (answer: no)', the Tories campaigned on immigration limits, high rates of crime and the NHS and also launched the slogan, 'It's not racist to impose limits on immigration'. Labour fought back strongly, attacking Michael Howard's time as Home Secretary under John Major under the logo, 'Britain's working, don't let the Tories wreck it again'. The Liberal Democrats meanwhile were fighting under Charles Kennedy, but the full extent of his problems with alcohol were coming to light, with the Lib Dem Leader appearing confused and uncertain at the party's launch.

The Lib Dems launched something they called a 'decapitation strategy', aiming to unseat five senior Tories: Michael Howard, Theresa May, David Davis (who was now Shadow Home Secretary), Shadow Chancellor Oliver Letwin and Tim Collins, the Shadow Education Secretary. This blew up in their face straight away: naming the five individuals actually had the effect of strengthening local support for them, and in the event only Tim Collins lost his seat – to Tim Farron, now himself head of the Lib Dems. Meanwhile Theresa increased her majority.

Come election day, Labour still got back in with a healthy majority, but the sheen really was beginning to wear off. They lost 46 seats and got in with 35.2 per cent of the vote, the lowest of any majority government in British history. The Tories gained 33 seats and with 32.4 per cent of the vote were not actually that far behind Labour, while the Lib Dems gained 11 seats. Michael Howard was actually deemed to have put in a highly creditable performance and while he might not have made it to Number 10, he had not only halted the party's decline but actually put it on track to start moving back towards power. But as so often in politics and elsewhere, it was to be someone else who was to seize the glittering prize.

Six months after the election Michael Howard stepped down as party leader, but before he did so, he made a major reshuffle of his front bench that paved the way for what was to come. A bright young backbencher called David Cameron had been Howard's special adviser. Howard promoted him to Shadow Secretary of State for Education and Skills. George Osborne, meanwhile, had been Shadow Chief Secretary to the Treasury: Howard bumped him up to Shadow Chancellor, a position he held until he became the real thing. He also had the satisfaction of being party leader when Blair suffered his first parliamentary defeat: the British government wanted to extend to 90 days the period that suspected terrorists could be held without charge.

Howard announced he would be leaving in May and actually stood down in December, giving the party plenty of time to pull itself together and consider what it was going to do next. There were four contenders for the leadership: David Cameron, David Davis, Liam Fox and Kenneth Clarke. When Cameron threw his hat into the ring in September, although senior colleagues including William Hague, George Osborne, Boris Johnson and Oliver Letwin supported him, he was still largely an unknown quantity and most people didn't think he had much of a chance. However, during the 2005 Tory Party Conference he gave an extremely well-received speech, delivered without notes, saying he wanted 'to switch on a whole new generation' and make people 'feel good about being Conservatives again'.

It was something of a game changer: the Tories were back.

11

GIRL POWER

When David Cameron and those who came to be known as the 'Notting Hill set' took over the party at the end of 2005, no one outside politics knew quite what to make of them. Unlike most of the electorate, they were rich, privileged and from semi-aristocratic backgrounds and yet these were the people charged with dragging the Tories kicking and screaming into the twenty-first century. They were of a type, public school followed by Oxbridge, and they were young. David Cameron was thirty-nine when he took over the leadership and forty-three when he became Prime Minister, the youngest person to hold the role since Lord Liverpool in 1812, beating the record set by Tony Blair. George Osborne became Shadow Chancellor at just thirty-three and then became the real thing, five years later.

Many of the men (and at the heart of the Notting Hill set, they *were* mainly men) around them were of a similar vintage and although this was presented to the public in an enormously positive light, this energetic generation of young people ready to steer the party back on track and reflecting the face of vibrant (but not diverse) youthful Britain, it meant that the Tories had essentially skipped a generation. Many of these people were newcomers to Parliament, let alone shadow government: Cameron became an MP in 2001, the same year Osborne and Boris Johnson got in, and Michael Gove, who was to be promoted very quickly, was even later, becoming an MP in 2005. In other words, the class of 1997, to which Theresa May belonged, had been leapfrogged. Some others of that era who had been expected to pursue brilliant careers fell by the wayside. Others imploded. Theresa simply kept her head down and got on.

David Cameron was on the whole a career politician but he had had a brief spell in PR, working as the director of corporate affairs at Carlton Communications, and so he was able to understand fully quite what low regard the Tories were held in at the time and set about doing something about it – 'detoxifying the brand', as the jargon had it. And so a range of initiatives was launched, which had the old guard choking on their sherry, including a speech to the Centre for Social Justice, which had been founded by Iain Duncan Smith.

'The fact is that the hoodie is a response to a problem, not a problem in itself,' proclaimed the future PM. 'We – the people in suits – often see hoodies as aggressive, the uniform of a rebel army of young gangsters. But, for young people, hoodies are often more defensive than offensive. They're a way to stay invisible in the street. In a dangerous environment the best thing to do is keep your head down, blend in; don't stand out. For some, the hoodie represents all that's wrong about youth culture in Britain today. For me, adult society's response to the hoodie shows how far we are from finding the long-term answers to put things right.'

There was a great deal more, most of it not on the subject of hoodies, but this became famously known as the PM's 'hug a hoodie' speech, even though he'd never actually used the phrase. Shortly afterwards he was pictured looking earnest while an actual hoodie made rude gestures in the background.

There was a lot more along these lines. Emphasising his environmental credentials – 'vote blue to go green' – Cameron risked and indeed received ridicule after he was pictured in April 2006 on a sledge drawn by huskies when he visited a remote Norwegian glacier to examine the effects of global warming.

Taking on those who thought the Tories were there only to protect the moneyed elite, he made a speech to the Google Zeitgeist Europe conference: 'It's time we admitted that there's more to life than money, and it's time we focused not just on GDP, but on GWB – general well-being. Well-being can't be measured by money or traded in markets. It's about the beauty of our surroundings, the quality of our culture and, above all, the strength of our relationships. Improving our society's sense of well-being is, I believe, the central political challenge of our times.'

The following year – 2007 – there was a trip to Rwanda to examine an aid project, which unfortunately took place at the same time as widespread flooding across the PM's south-west constituency, drawing criticism that he wasn't looking after the people who needed him back home. And so it went on. Cameron was pictured cycling through the capital on his way to work (embarrassingly, a car carrying all his papers was spotted behind him). Already he had taken paternity leave when his daughter Florence was born in 2006 and widely flaunted his 'new man' credentials in every possible way except for when it came to getting on with female voters, who never warmed to him, and generally hammered home the fact that he was a new type of Tory, that the party was not made up of self-interested old fogeys and that they were ready to lead the country once more.

Of course this didn't go down well with everyone: Lord Tebbit compared him to the Cambodian tyrant Pol Pot, 'intent on purging even the memory of Thatcherism before building a New Modern Compassionate Green Globally Aware Party'. Then Quentin Davies MP defected from the Conservatives to Labour on 26 June 2007, saying Cameron was 'superficial, unreliable and [with] an apparent lack of any clear convictions'. The PM was widely mocked when it became known that family and friends called him 'Dave' and in 2008, in a bizarre episode, David Davis, then Shadow Home Secretary, announced that he was going to resign as an MP and then stand again in the subsequent by-election, a move taken as a direct challenge to Cameron's authority. In the event he was re-elected but he was on the backbenches for years after that – his own choice, for Cameron did ask him to join the government.

But Theresa, who was playing a long game, participated in none of this. She could rightly claim to have been one of the party's earliest modernisers and so what she did do was address the biggest issue of the lot of them: the lack of women in the party. The problem was highlighted by a potential Tory candidate called Laura Sandys: subsequently the MP for South Thanet, she made the news in 2005 after applying to fourteen constituencies and making the shortlist for two of them. For what it is worth, she was a well-connected Tory, at that: her father was Duncan Sandys, who through his first marriage had been Winston Churchill's son-in-law and was made a life peer. If a woman with her sort of connections couldn't get on, then who could?

The problem was sufficiently pressing – and David Cameron certainly recognised that although, not yet leader, he didn't actually sign up to the campaign – a group of senior Conservative women formed a new lobby group called Women2Win, which aimed for half of the top 100 winnable seats to be contested by women. It was the brainchild of a number of formidable movers and shakers, among them

Shireen Ritchie, a leading Tory councillor in Kensington and Chelsea, who attracted the most attention at the time because her stepson, Guy, was then married to one of the most high-profile women in the world: singer-songwriter Madonna. It was launched in November 2005, shortly before the Tory leadership results were announced.

Other big names were Anne (now Baroness) Jenkin, who was married to the distinguished Tory Eurosceptic MP Bernard Jenkin, and of course Theresa herself. 'If we don't do something now, we are going to lose out and carry on losing out,' she warned at the launch. 'There seems to be a new militancy to try to sort this out. A lot of constituencies still have a stereotypical view of what an MP should be – and that is often male. You may have thought that having Margaret Thatcher [as leader] would have broken that down, but part of the problem is that many men saw her as an honorary man – "one of us", so to speak.'

Elsewhere she commented, 'It is a little-known fact that there are more men in the shadow cabinet called David than there are women. Women2Win are making this challenge to the leadership candidates: over the course of the remaining leadership election campaign, make clear your commitment to reform the Conservative Party into a party that represents, reflects and understands Britain today.'

In total six shadow cabinet members had already signed up to the declaration: Theresa, Caroline Spelman, David Willetts, Oliver Letwin, Michael Ancram and Andrew Lansley, while it was supported by a number of Tory MPs, including Peter Viggers, Maria Miller, Bernard Jenkin and Peter Lilley. Katherine Rake, chairman of the Fawcett Society, which works for increased women's representation in Parliament, spoke at the launch: the overall picture was 'pretty dire,' she said, in the Conservative Party in terms of women's representation. 'The party looks outdated to an electorate that expects women to have equal opportunities in the workplace and in public life.' Figures released by the campaign showed that in 1932 there were thirteen Conservative women MPs. At the last election, seventy-three years later, the total was still just seventeen. Women make up just 9 per cent of the Parliamentary Conservative Party, an increase of just 1 per cent on the 2001 General Election total. According to the campaign, at the current rate it will take the Conservative Party four hundred years to achieve equal representation of women within its ranks.

'The system is not currently operating on merit,' noted Dr Rake. 'There is discrimination right the way through the system, whether knowing or unknowing. What we are suggesting is positive action that allows women a fair chance, but within a competitive framework.'

This initiative was at least as important as all the hoodie-hugging and husky-sledging, if not more so, because the party was finally beginning to face up to the fact that it was no longer the preserve of white, middle-aged men. In many ways, it bears comparison with Tony Blair and Gordon Brown and the New Labour project, because there was the realisation there had to be a break from the past. With Cameron as a fresh-faced new leader, complete with a personable young wife, Samantha, who like so many women had to juggle the demands of working in a business and bringing up her family, and a new set of Tories in charge, there was the scent of change in the air.

It was beginning to become apparent that the Iraq invasion was turning into a disaster of unforeseen proportions and with the Conservatives looking fresher than they had done for decades, matters were looking far more positive for the party. One aspect of this, of course, was that none of the people now in charge had played any part in the political assassination of Margaret Thatcher. No matter how good a candidate the Ken Clarkes and Michael Howards of this world might be, the fact remained that both had played a part in her downfall (although Howard was a strong supporter) and as such they would be forever tainted with what had gone before. None of this applied to the current crowd.

Under David Cameron's leadership of the Tories while in Opposition, Theresa continued to serve in a variety of shadow roles, which performed the dual task of helping her to learn about individual governmental departments while teaching her that life was pretty miserable when you had no power to implement your ideas. Cameron first made her Shadow Leader of the House of Commons, a role she held for four years, and then Shadow Secretary of State for Work and Pensions. She never served as a shadow in the Home Office, however, nor indeed in any of the great offices of state, the others being Shadow Chancellor, Shadow Foreign Minister and of course, Leader of the Opposition.

The Tories unveiled their new agenda at the beginning of 2006: it consisted of six pledges to help the poor, look after the environment, stand up to the police and big business, promote economic stability (memories of Black Wednesday were beginning to fade, but only just) and the NHS must be improved. The brains behind all this were the central cast of 'Cameroons': Dave himself, George Osborne, Francis Maude, Oliver Letwin, strategist Steve Hilton (who would later campaign for Leave in the 2016 referendum) and George Bridges, the party's research chief. Theresa was not in that inner circle but credit must go to her for having started the whole process off: although many had not forgiven her for the 'nasty party' speech, others felt that she, rather than those who came after her and snatched the political limelight (for the time being), was the person who recognised the full extent to which the Tories had to change.

As the years wore on, however, she was given remarkably little credit for her foresight. Attention continued to focus on her shoes and her hair; the Democratic Party nominee Hillary Clinton once mused that if she wanted to make the front pages, all she had to do was change her hairstyle. Theresa didn't get the front page, more somewhere around the middle, but she did excite speculation every time there was evidence of a new style. Was she trying to warm up, perhaps shed the ice queen style? Just what did it mean? Theresa played up to the shoe obsession with a good enough humour – when you are required to wear a metaphorical coat of armour most of the time, light relief needs to be taken where it can be found – 'Normally when people ask me how many shoes I have, my answer is "not enough", she told *The Times*. 'I must have roughly double the average, around forty pairs. I'm not sure about a favourite, but I do still have a pair of those leopard-print ones that hit the headlines a few years ago. I've never had a pair of Manolo Blahniks or Jimmy Choos – that's what I'd treat myself to if I won the lottery.'

That was canny – allying herself to those who played the lottery as their only chance of getting out of a rut. Theresa of course had genuinely humble origins, but it was also clear that she didn't want to be identified with the new moneyed elite. She followed that up by attending a Women2Win champagne reception at a branch of the shoe and clothing store L.K. Bennett, where goods were offered to female Tory MPs at a 20 per cent discount. Theresa nabbed a pair of blue ankle boots. She also became one of a number of high-profile women who posed in a T-shirt bearing the slogan, 'This is what a feminist looks like' – something Margaret Thatcher would not have dreamed of doing. Nor would David Cameron, although he was asked.

Theresa, who unlike so many of her colleagues had had a job in the real world, was also aware that other areas of life had to change. Flexible working was one cause she championed, although she was keen to make the point that this was an issue that affected both sexes. 'Flexible working is not just for women with children,' she told *The Guardian* in December 2009. 'It is necessary at the other end of the scale. If people can move into part-time work, instead of retirement, then that will be a huge help. If people can fit their work around caring responsibilities for the elderly, the disabled, then again that's very positive.'

She also had to put up with frequent speculation that she was to be moved from her job (admittedly every senior Tory, with the possible exception of George Osborne, got this). On 1 October 2006 she turned fifty, an event marked by a quiet dinner with Philip, putting her very much on the more senior side of the shadow cabinet, but despite evidence of worship of youth among senior Tories that would have done former PM Tony Blair proud, no one actually believed the rumours she was to be pushed aside. Increasingly it was becoming apparent that Theresa did not just have ability and experience, she had gravitas too. That quality was important in any politician, especially in a woman in a party so short on women.

The Cameron-led new era continued when at the 2006 annual conference he told the party it had better get used to gay marriage and single mothers, something no one appeared to take very seriously, given the shock when it actually happened. Theresa, meanwhile, was beginning to encounter topics that would take up a good deal of her time when she was finally in office: in November 2006 she warned of growing public anger about the fact that the terrorist suspect Abu Hamza had been allowed to make a fortune from a property transaction while in prison – the British government had supposedly frozen his assets but he had still been able to transfer a flat into the ownership of his son. There was criticism of the government for failing to deport foreign criminals. Then there were continuing, and at that stage totally unsuccessful, attempts to hold Tony Blair to account over Iraq.

The New Year wore on, with a row in February 2007 over whether or not David Cameron had smoked cannabis while at school – 'I think politicians are entitled to a private past,' said Theresa, who had absolutely nothing to be embarrassed about in hers. 'I think that's right. Most of us go into politics because we become interested in becoming politicians. We are not spending our whole youth thinking, well, I might be a Member of Parliament therefore I'm going to be extremely careful about what I'm doing in particular areas.'

One of the few occasions in which Theresa was almost touched by scandal happened that year when it transpired that her previous personal trainer, Lee Waite, was given six years for drug dealing, but then of course it turned out not only did Theresa not have a clue about his nefarious activities – no one was ever foolish enough even to pretend to think that she did – but that his employer, the David Lloyd Club, didn't have the first idea about it either. Theresa was not available for comment, but why should she have been? The furore all died down soon enough.

The real political development that year concerned the Labour Party, when the brooding Chancellor Gordon Brown finally managed to force Tony Blair out of Number 10 and take up residence there himself. After a brief honeymoon period, it soon became very clear that the premiership of the 'Son of the Manse' was to be a disaster, starting with a botched episode in which Brown allowed speculation to mount that he was going to hold a snap election and then decided not to do so, after all. George Osborne, in a stroke of political genius that has still not been acted upon, promised to increase the inheritance tax threshold to £1 million, a move greeted so enthusiastically by the public that Brown's nerve failed.

It looked like a clear act of political cowardice from which he never recovered, followed by a more unexpected development – despite having connived his entire life for the top job, he turned out not only to be temperamentally unsuited to the role but also out of his depth. In marked contrast to when Theresa also took over from a sitting prime minister and appeared almost immediately to be born to the job, Brown floundered. The rages became more volcanic; the Tory nose lifted further up and scented something that felt even more like victory in the air.

In 2008, Lehman Brothers bank filed for bankruptcy, triggering a global financial crisis that changed the political landscape and reverberates to this day. Gordon Brown, the man who once promised 'an end to boom and bust', was caught off balance and viciously turned on his own Chancellor, Alistair

Darling, when he correctly forecast that a major recession was on its way. More annual conferences came and went. The following year saw the MPs' expenses scandal, which ended several parliamentary careers and even resulted in criminal charges in a few cases. It was a massive blow to MPs' reputations with the public as one sordid detail after another began to slip out: claims on expenses for cleaning duck houses and moats; claims on expenses for porn films, for paying family members and nannies, for paying mortgage interest on properties with no mortgage, for 'flipping' houses between the constituency and London in order to claim for purchasing and avoid Capital Gains Tax (CGT). MPs also claimed for sofas and widescreen televisions, for extensions to their houses, for photoshoots for political pamphlets, for plants for the garden and, in one case, for a 59p box of matches. All the parties were involved; disgust was distributed equally. No one came out of it well.

Almost no one, that is. Theresa was one of the few MPs completely untouched by the scandal: there was never a hint or suggestion that she had done anything untoward or even a little unwise.

'Over the past four years she has claimed just over £15,000 for a flat in London while her designated main home is in her Maidenhead constituency. The claims have been for mortgage interest on her designated second home in London,' wrote the *Daily Telegraph*, the paper which broke the expenses claims story, in June 2009, adding she was 'one of the most modest expense claimants in Parliament'.

Financial probity was another quality that could be added to the list. (Another two senior Tories untouched by the furore were Philip Hammond and Michael Gove; meanwhile Tony Blair's expenses claims were shredded 'by mistake' before anyone could have a good look.)

As 2010, and the next General Election approached, Theresa, now Shadow Work and Pensions Secretary, ploughed on. Two types of stories originated about her at this stage: either she was about to be promoted as one of the few competent senior Tory women around or she was to be demoted because she had such a low profile. And that was true. While kitten heels still appeared in the papers when picture editors were low on alternative choices – indeed, at one point she even sported some leopard-skin wellies – and Theresa bobbed up regularly from behind the parapet to attack Labour on whatever they were doing now, she did and said very little that generated major headlines. The Women2Win initiative might be promoting the cause of women in Parliament, but it was not generally recognised by the wider public. There was the occasional speculation (including from Michael Gove) that Theresa might one day be a leader, but this was the Cameron era and no one saw the spectacular coup that was to propel her to power six years hence.

And perhaps they should have done because Theresa was actually deploying exactly the same tactic she was to use with such devastating impact again: she kept her head down, didn't join in any of the factions, kept her powder dry and bided her time. She had twice experienced what could happen if you made waves of the wrong sort: the first time in that 'nasty party' speech, which was still brought up and very often held against her by Tories furious that she had provided their enemies with a convenient label. Theresa, never a slow learner, clearly realised that it was better not to grab the headlines if the end result was that everyone felt you were doing your party down. Her other experience, of course, was that she had been in the pro-Portillo faction in the previous leadership race and had seen up close what damage differing sides of the same party could do to one another.

She might have seemed modest and unassuming on the outside, which indeed she was, but she was also a remarkably canny political operator. And she was in it for the long game.

12

NEW WORLD ORDER

The circumstances surrounding the General Election of 2010 were unusual. For a start, the three major parties had all changed leaders since the previous outing: David Cameron had replaced Michael Howard, Gordon Brown had deposed Tony Blair and the Lib Dems were on their second successor to Charles Kennedy, after Nick Clegg replaced Menzies 'Ming' Campbell. None of the three leaders had ever fronted a general election campaign before.

Public disillusionment with Labour was now firmly entrenched. The bright promises of yesteryear had given way to two outstanding issues: recession and the Iraq War. The 'straight kinda guy' was off promoting his own interests, although the full extent to which Blair intended to build up his own fortune was not yet apparent and he did put in a few appearances on the campaign trail, and Gordon Brown had proved a disaster as Prime Minister. In the run-up to the election he was caught on air calling Gillian Duffy, a Labour supporter from Rochdale, a 'bigoted woman' when she challenged him on the issue of immigration: 'You can't say anything about the immigrants because you're saying that you're . . . but all these Eastern Europeans what are coming in, where are they flocking from?' she demanded to know.

'A million people have come from Europe, but a million British people have gone into Europe,' Brown replied.

But afterwards, his exchange with his communications director, Justin Forsyth, was overheard when the pair failed to realise the microphone was still on:

'That was a disaster,' said Brown. 'Sue [Nye, his director of government relations] should never have put me with that woman. Whose idea was that?'

'I don't know, I didn't see her,' replied Forsyth.

'Sue's, I think. Just ridiculous . . .'

'What did she say?'

'Everything, she was just a sort of bigoted woman who said she used to be Labour. I mean, it's just ridiculous. Sue pushed her up towards me.'

Despite a subsequent public apology, Brown never really recovered from that and nor did it help when Manish Sood, Labour candidate for the Tory-held seat of North West

Norfolk, described him as Britain's worst ever prime minister, a claim he repeated several times, thus entirely diverting attention away from a speech Brown made to Citizens UK, described by commentators as his best speech of the campaign.

The run-up to the big day was marred by any number of odd events. The UKIP leader Nigel Farage was injured when a light aircraft he was travelling in crashed; the police were called in when it emerged that some people who were listed on the electoral register of the London Borough of Tower Hamlets did not actually exist. A Labour candidate in Moray, Stuart MacLennan, was sacked after referring to elderly voters as 'coffin dodgers' and voters in the north of Scotland as 'teuchters', which he swiftly followed up by publicly insulting a number of figures, including Cameron, Clegg, John Bercow and the Labour MP Diane Abbott. The Tories proved that there was also room for arrant stupidity in their own party when Philip Lardner, Conservative candidate for North Ayrshire, made offensive remarks about homosexuality on his website. He was suspended but still appeared on the ballot paper because it was too late to remove his name. For the first time ever the leaders of the three main parties took part in a televised debate: Nick Clegg did far better than expected and his performance was almost certainly the reason his party performed well at the polls. Disquiet was voiced in some quarters about the fact that so few women seemed to be playing a major role in the national debate and while Theresa fought with her usual mix of reliability and rectitude, she certainly didn't stand out at the time.

On Thursday, 6 May 2010 the nation went out to vote and returned a hung parliament, the first since 1974 and only the second since World War II. The Conservatives had actually managed a 5.1 per cent swing away from Labour, quite close to Margaret Thatcher's 5.3 per cent swing of 1979, but it was not enough to ensure a majority. The Tories would have needed 326 seats but actually fell 20 short. It was quickly apparent that a coalition government was on the cards and after a brief, doomed attempt on the part of Gordon Brown to form an alliance between Labour and the Lib Dems, which was condemned by some of his own MPs, the Tories and the Lib Dems began talks in earnest.

Brown resigned as PM on 11 May, bringing to an end thirteen years of Labour in power, Cameron stepped into his shoes and just after midnight on 12 May, it was announced that a deal had been struck with the Lib Dems. And so for the first time ever, a coalition government became the direct result of the choices made by the electorate, David Cameron began a political 'bromance' that was to end in disaster for the Lib Dems, and the Labour Party started on its long march to electoral oblivion.

As is always the case in the first days after an election, the new Prime Minister went into seclusion with his confidantes and advisers and began allocating governmental roles, although one problem was caused by the fact that the Lib

Dems were now their partner in government and so not everyone who had served in the Shadow Cabinet was going to make it to the real thing. There was no surprise when George Osborne became Chancellor and little wonder when William Hague was made Foreign Secretary and First Secretary of State. The redoubtable Kenneth Clarke stepped into the role of Lord Chancellor. There was some considerable interest, however, when Theresa May became the second woman, after the lamentable Jacqui Smith, to be named as Home Secretary. She was also the fourth woman to hold one of the great offices of state after, in this order, Margaret Thatcher, Margaret Beckett, who had been Foreign Secretary, and Smith. It was a big promotion: up from a middle-ranking position into one of the great offices of state, and it was done at the expense of Chris Grayling, who had been Shadow Home Secretary and hadn't made much of a mark. Elsewhere, nine members of the thirty-two strong Shadow Cabinet didn't make it into government and another six were to attend without being full members.

A notoriously difficult brief, the Home Office had been a death sentence for many a promising career and Theresa was not taking over at a propitious time (indeed, such a time never exists). With a remit covering the police, immigration, drugs policy, extremism, deportation of undesirables and of course the isolated incidents that comprise 'events, dear boy, events', among much else, elephant traps lay everywhere and it takes a skilled politician to negotiate this terrain for even a short time, let alone six years. Among the problems waiting in the in-tray were a proposed cap on skilled migrants entering Britain from outside the EU, scrapping ID cards and ending the collection of DNA profiles, negotiating with the police over Tory plans for elected police commissioners and tackling the growing problem of Islamic extremism. Theresa, as might be expected, didn't turn a hair.

There were three more women in the Cabinet: Caroline Spelman, who was Secretary of State for Environment, Food and Rural Affairs, Cheryl Gillan, the Secretary of State for Wales, and Lady Warsi, Minister without Portfolio and the first Muslim to sit as a full voting member of the Cabinet. Nick Clegg became Deputy Prime Minister and four other Lib Dems were in attendance.

Theresa is one of the most pragmatic politicians of her generation as her voting record was to show over the next few years and an early indication of this came now. When in opposition she had voted against the repeal of Section 28 and she had also not been present in the Chamber when the vote on civil partnerships went through. She had also voted to reduce the time limit on abortions and to strengthen the laws regarding the 'need for a father', where IVF treatment was concerned. As a vicar's daughter and a practising Christian, they were perhaps issues she felt a little delicate about.

But there was to be no more doubt on this score: 'Certainly there were some votes I wasn't present for,' she told Channel 4 News. 'But what we intend to do in government is taking forward an agenda on equalities across the whole range of equalities,' she added. 'In this particular issue we have some very real commitments, for example in terms of homophobic bullying in schools.' As she had also been made Minister of Equalities, which encompassed gay rights as well as women's, this was the line she would be taking from now on.

There was some objection, though, from Lesbian, Gay, Bisexual, Transgender (LGBT) groups, because she had also voted against greater adoption rights for gay couples: indeed the pragmatic politician dealt with the issue head-on. 'On gay adoption I have changed my mind because I have been persuaded that when you are looking at the future for a child, I think it's better for a child who is perhaps in an institutional environment, if they have an opportunity of being in a stable, family environment – be that a heterosexual couple or a gay couple – then I think it's more important that that child is in that stable and loving environment and I have genuinely changed my mind on that,' she said on an edition of BBC1's *Question Time* in May 2010. She followed that up by writing an article in *Pink News* about the need to tackle homophobia in sport: 'Cultural change is not straightforward, but it is essential to advance the cause of LGB and T rights,' she noted. 'Of course there is a role for politicians here too and I'm proud that this election saw an increase in the number of openly gay MPs in Parliament, although we have further to go.'

She then launched a document setting out the coalition

government's promises on gay and trans rights, including allowing gay people to have religious civil partnerships and removing historical convictions for consensual gay sex from criminal records.

At the Home Office, Theresa hit the ground running, comprehensively showing her mettle and wiping out any doubts that she might not be up to the job – quite the reverse. She first turned her attention to the subject of national identity cards: the increasingly authoritarian Labour Party had been on the verge of introducing them, as well as reforms to the database scheme, both anathema to a Britain where identity papers had never been required before. The announcement that the ID card scheme would be scrapped was made within weeks; it was to reverse 'the substantial erosion of civil liberties' in recent years, the Home Office announced.

Theresa also announced renewed safeguards on the retention of people's DNA: 'We are absolutely clear we need to make some changes in relation to the DNA database,' she said. 'For example one of the first things we will do is to ensure that all the people who have actually been convicted of a crime and are not present on it are actually on the DNA database. The last government did not do that. It focused on retaining the DNA data of people who were innocent. Let's actually make sure that those who have been found guilty are actually on that database.'

For all her pragmatism, however, Theresa was intent on showing that she was her own woman and that meant she wasn't kowtowing to anyone, even the mighty USA. That same month, just weeks after the election, she became embroiled in the row about Gary McKinnon. McKinnon was a somewhat troubled man who had hacked into computers belonging to the US military and NASA between February 2001 and March 2002; he never denied this but said merely that he was looking around out of curiosity and because the systems' security was so bad. The enraged American authorities had been trying to extradite him for some time. However there were real fears as to his mental health, especially as he has been diagnosed with Asperger's syndrome. There were also doubts about whether he'd receive a fair trial. The fight was not yet over but Theresa immediately announced that the deportation would be adjourned.

Another issue was with the Labour-introduced registration scheme for carers of young children and the vulnerable, which had been established in the wake of the dreadful murders of two schoolgirls, Holly Wells and Jessica Chapman, by the school caretaker Ian Huntley in 2002. While that case had provoked horror and revulsion, the plans had gone much too far, to the extent that people visiting schools to talk to children were to be registered. The bestselling author Philip Pullman had called them 'ludicrous and insulting'; Theresa clearly agreed. The measures were 'draconian,' she told the BBC. 'You were assumed to be guilty until you were proven innocent, and told you were able to work with children. All sorts of groups out there were deeply concerned about this and how it was going to affect them. There were schools where they were very concerned that foreign exchanges could be finished as a result of this, parents were worried about looking after other people's children after school.'

Greater attention, perhaps, was focused on the love-in still going on between the two young party leaders as they chased each other around Downing Street's rose garden, but what Theresa was doing mirrored the efforts of the Conservative Party as a whole. She was trying to re-establish individual freedoms while at the same time clamping down on those who were clearly a menace to society – or worse – while at the same time being unafraid to take on established interests such as the police. The previous Labour administration had become increasingly authoritarian in tone, trying to pass legislation that infringed on the population's historic freedoms while at the same time, bizarrely, allowing people into the country who posed a threat. Theresa was trying to reverse this process. She spoke out about a court decision to allow two suspected terrorists to remain in the UK on the grounds that they might face torture in Pakistan, a decision that provoked widespread outrage, not least from the Home Office.

The first major crisis to occur on her watch was the so-called 'Cumbria shootings', in which a gunman, Derrick Bird, went on the rampage on 2 June 2010, killing twelve people and injuring eleven others before turning the gun on himself. One of the worst killing sprees in British history, Bird, a fifty-two-year old taxi driver, started his murderous campaign when he left his home in Rowrah and drove to his twin brother David's home in Lamplugh, where he shot him. His next victim was the family solicitor Kevin Commons, after which he targeted other taxi drivers and finally people at random before finally walking into the woods and shooting himself.

It has never really been clear what turned him into a monster: previously described as a 'quiet, popular' man, there were reports, never confirmed, that he had in the past sought treatment for mental illness, that he had been involved in a family dispute over his father's will, which would have explained the targeting of his brother and solicitor, that he was under investigation for tax evasion by the Inland Revenue and even that he had been in a relationship with a Thai girl and had taken it badly when she finished with him. Whatever had happened to him, it resulted in a dreadful tragedy.

It was one of those events that deeply shocked the entire nation. The Queen paid tribute to the victims, Prince Charles visited the area, as did both David Cameron and Theresa May, who toured the area, visited some of the victims in hospital and spoke to the local police. Theresa was also called upon to make a statement about it in the House of Commons. This happened less than a month into the new coalition government and it can only be said that both Prime Minister and Home Secretary acted as they were called upon to do, reflecting the gravity of the situation, marking the tragedy with their presence, assuring the population that this was a one-off incident in that Britain has very strict gun-control laws. Both understood the need for this.

'People – I have met some – are having to come to terms with the most appalling random acts they will find very difficult to understand and in some cases there will be no proper explanation,' said the Prime Minister. 'Inevitably, people will have questions and the Government needs to be here to listen, to show them that it cares and also to try and find the right way to answer the questions that people legitimately have.'

Theresa was so far coping with the role and as ghastly as these events had been, there was no time to brood. There was still a huge amount to cope with elsewhere. The highly controversial Indian Muslim preacher Zakir Naik had been due to visit the UK to give a series of lectures in London and Sheffield. Peace TV, which employed him, described him as 'a medical doctor by professional training and a dynamic international orator on Islam and comparative religion. Dr Naik clarifies Islamic viewpoints and clears misconceptions about Islam using the Koran.'

Others deemed him a troublemaker and Theresa agreed, using her powers as Home Secretary to ban him from the UK. 'Numerous comments made by Dr Naik are evidence to me of his unacceptable behaviour,' she said. 'Coming to the UK is a privilege, not a right, and I am not willing to allow those who might not be conducive to the public good to enter the UK. Exclusion powers are very serious and no decision is taken lightly or as a method of stopping open debate on issues.'

This was music to the ears of the many who were increasingly concerned about who exactly was allowed to come into the country, although it was one small and isolated incident in the ocean of problems Theresa and the Home Office had to face when it came to the issue of visitors to the UK. However, it was also a measure of her inner steel. Reports emerged that Sabin Khan, an adviser in the Home Office's Office of Security and Counter Terrorism, had been very critical of the new Home Secretary in private, adding that she and the Office's Director General, Charles Farr, were 'gutted and mortified' by the ban. The upshot of this was that Khan was suspended from her job and the ensuing row provoked a letter from the Conservative MPs Nicholas Boles, Angie Bray, Robert Halfon and Richard Harrington. They 'warmly endorse the courageous decision' by Mrs May to ban Dr Naik, they wrote, and were 'deeply disturbed to learn from authoritative reports that some senior civil servants within the Home Office's Office of Security and Counter Terrorism criticised Theresa May's brave move. It is vital that the Office of Security and Counter Terrorism employs personnel at all levels who have the necessary objectivity to fulfil their tasks. It is essential, therefore, that the Home Secretary is able to enjoy the loyalty of those working for her. If civil servants cannot give that, they must reconsider their positions.'

Another example of that inner steel came when Theresa

met the Security Minister Dame Pauline Neville-Jones shortly after the coalition government had got under way. Theresa asked for an update on counter-terrorism measures and it is hard to know whether the answer she received was rude, arrogant, foolish, hubristic or all four, but it is alleged it went something like this: 'I'm sorry, Home Secretary, but I'm afraid I can't talk to you about that, because you don't have the security clearance.'

Theresa was by all accounts so stunned by this that she didn't reply, although the look she gave in return would have done a gorgon proud, but from that moment on, Lady Neville-Jones didn't have a hope. The two clashed repeatedly and unpleasantly over and again throughout the course of the next year, until matters between them got to such a pitch that the Baroness went to the Prime Minister and demanded to be allowed to report directly to him and not to the Home Secretary. Cameron turned her down flat and in May 2011 she resigned. By contrast Theresa denied any rift and spoke warmly of her work, claiming they had a 'good working relationship'. At any rate, Lady Neville-Jones was gone and the working relationship was no more.

There was a predictable outcry from some outposts of big business when Theresa then announced that she was pressing ahead with plans to cap non-EU immigration into Britain, but it had been a policy that had swayed some wavering voters and she wanted to push it through. She encountered opposition from within the party, namely Michael Gove and

David Willetts, who were concerned that it might send a 'negative signal'. In the event she was forced to water down the proposals but still pressed ahead.

Another attempt to get rid of Labour's obsession with micro-management came when Theresa scrapped a ten-point police pledge to ensure that officers spent at least 80 per cent of their time on the beat, but she did so in a speech that also announced budget cuts and made it clear she expected them to do their jobs. She told the Association of Police Officers that 'front line availability should increase even as budgets contract' and that she was planning for locally elected police commissioners.

This was followed up with proposals for a fundamental review of the previous Labour government's security and counter-terrorism legislation, including 'stop and search' powers, announced in July, and her intention to review the 28-day limit on detaining terrorist suspects without charge. Later that month she announced a further package of reforms to policing in England and Wales in the House of Commons, which would replace Labour's central crime agency, SOCA (Serious Organised Crime Agency), with a new National Crime Agency and, following the Conservative Party 2010 General Election manifesto's flagship proposal for a 'Big Society' based on voluntary action, she also proposed increasing the role of civilian 'reservists' for crime control.

Later that month, continuing to get rid of much of the Labour government's unsuccessful dross, Theresa proposed to abolish the Antisocial Behaviour Order (ASBO), which had not only been useless but had come to be worn as a badge of pride: almost half of ASBOs had been breached between 2000 and 2008, leading to 'fast-track' criminal convictions. She suggested a less punitive, community-based approach to tackling social disorder, eliciting complaints from former Labour home secretaries David Blunkett (who introduced ASBOs) and Alan Johnson – but there was nothing they could do. 'We need to make anti-social behaviour what it once was – unusual, abnormal and something to stand up to – instead of what it has become: frequent, normal and tolerated,' Theresa declared.

In December 2010, the year closed to the tune of violent rioting in central London by students objecting to increased tuition fees. There was particular concern when a car containing Prince Charles and the Duchess of Cornwall got caught up in the mayhem and was targeted by the hooligans present, something which put Theresa's own position at risk as the couple's safety should have been paramount with the police. There were calls for an inquiry, subsequently ignored, but it was a serious misstep at the start of what had been a very good tenure. In the event, of course, Theresa survived. She toyed with the idea of allowing the police to use water cannons if matters got so badly out of hand again, a suggestion she later backed down from, but she was making it obvious she was no pushover.

The upshot of all this was that by the year end, Theresa was seeing off her political opponents, making it absolutely clear she would not tolerate insurrection from her ministers or civil servants, was only too happy to get rid of ineffectual Labour legislation (and there was a lot of it), and was not afraid of taking on the police. The Home Secretary was 'getting tough on crime and tough on the causes of crime', to use a famous phrase by someone who had never done either and she was attempting to crack down on immigration too. And all the while those kitten heels were successfully deflecting attention away from the fact that she had anything but a kittenish nature. All in all, it wasn't such a bad start.

13

THERESA'S PEOPLE

One of the reasons why Theresa May's tenure at the Home Office was so much longer and more successful than the vast majority of her predecessors is that she surrounded herself with a close coterie of skilful advisers and listened to them, usually more than she did her fellow politicians. Late nights working through ministerial red boxes with her small team were the norm – a modus operandi that drew comparisons with Gordon Brown, although as someone once pointed out when this was voiced, 'Theresa is at least a human being.'

While the former PM was given to volcanic rages, Theresa would go in the opposite direction, maintaining an icy silence when she was displeased (and often when she wasn't) until whoever else was in the room would start babbling inanely, losing ground, self-respect and indeed the argument. Unusually for a politician, she did not concern herself with attempting to form political alliances, schmoozing the Commons tea room or propping up one of the numerous taxpayer-subsidised bars and she was not afraid to pick fights with her colleagues, of which more later.

However, the other slightly odd comparison with Brown is that it was not unheard of for unnamed colleagues to go on the attack when they or Theresa were displeased. She is very good at defending her own territory and getting her own way, as quite a few of her ministerial colleagues found out to their cost, and if someone incurs her displeasure, she is not afraid to act, sometimes causing a huge rumpus in the background. The image of her being over-cautious is utterly wrong, as witnessed as far back as the comments over the 'nasty party', which continued to dog her even now.

In 2011 there was a great deal of bitterness surrounding an episode involving Brodie Clark, the £130,000-a-year head of the UK Border Agency, when he was accused of relaxing passport and anti-terror checks at Heathrow without Theresa's permission. Clark was duly suspended and the Home Office issued a statement: 'Instead, Brodie Clark is alleged to have authorised UKBA officials to abandon biometric checks on non-EEA (European Economic Area) nationals, the verification of the fingerprints of non-EEA nationals and warnings index checks on adults at Calais'. A source said that Theresa's reaction was 'incredulity and fury', that the border agency was a 'massive problem' and so it went on.

Clark was beside himself, telling MPs he was 'no rogue

officer. Nothing could be further from the truth', he had done nothing to 'enlarge, extend or redefine in any way' trials that were being run and added for good measure, 'Over forty years I have built up a reputation and over two days that reputation has been destroyed and I believe that has been largely from the contributions made by the Home Secretary.' In the end he resigned and received a payout, thought to be around £100,000, though the figure was not made public, with neither side admitting fault.

The statement put out was a masterpiece of obfuscation: 'Mr Clark remains at one with the objective of the Home Office in its efforts to maintain the security of the UK's border and he wishes his ex-colleagues every future success as they deal with the challenges of this demanding and vital business. The Home Office, in recognising Mr Clark's notable contribution to public life over a long period, wishes him every success for the future. Both Mr Clark and the Home Office are saddened by the events that took place in November 2011. Mr Clark and the Home Office believe that reaching a settlement is right and that it will ensure that the focus is correctly maintained on future border security. ' Nonetheless it was an unpleasant episode and one at odds with the saintliness that Theresa sometimes emanates: the steel within sometimes glints through.

She can also be very sharp-tongued. Of Kenneth Clarke (who later was overheard describing her as a 'bloody difficult woman'), she remarked acidly, 'I lock them up and he lets them out.' Of her colleagues in general, she commented,

'Like Indiana Jones, I don't like snakes – though that might lead some to ask why I'm in politics.' When in a toe-curling display of fatuousness, Miriam Clegg, Nick's wife, said, 'My very last question is: that little girl who is somewhere there, is she dreaming of becoming the next British Prime Minister?', Theresa replied, 'She's dreaming of carrying on doing a good job in the Home Office.'

It could be seen that her preoccupation with her wardrobe and the sometimes eccentric choices she makes are a way of detracting from the toughness – after all, anyone who likes frocks can't be as frightening as that. 'As a woman I know you can be very serious about something and very soberly dressed but add a little bit of interest with footwear,' she once said. 'I always tell women "you have to be yourself, don't assume you have to fit into a stereotype" and if your personality is shown through your clothes or shoes, so be it.'

But those who know her well say that the opposite is the case: because Theresa has such a reputation for being cautious, those wild and wacky Vivienne Westwood outfits are a way of showing that she is not afraid to take risks.

'She refuses to apologise for her success,' her former spin doctor, Katie Perrior, told *The Spectator*. 'She wears the clothes to show she is not the person you think she is. Her dress sense shows that risk-taking side. They are hidden signals. Her two fingers, a bit of control she has over her life.'

The three most influential people to work with Theresa, then and now, are Fiona Hill (formerly Cunningham before her divorce), Nick Timothy, both of whom Theresa appointed as Joint Downing Street Chief of Staff when she assumed office, and Stephen Parkinson. With Theresa in charge, this was the quartet that really ran the Home Office. Fiona Hill was responsible for everything from counter-terrorism policy to choice of footwear. A formidable figure, who described her boss as a 'lioness', she previously worked for Sky News and *The Scotsman* newspaper and led the work that resulted in the Modern Slavery Act, which was implemented in 2015. This garnered praise from an unexpected quarter: *The Voice* newspaper, which represents the black community, commented that she was 'fast becoming someone who the black and minority community can do business with' – which is not something it has said much in the past about a Conservative Home Secretary.

The Slavery Act was one of Theresa's most important achievements at the Home Office, the first act of its kind in Europe and one of the first in the world, establishing an independent Anti-Slavery Commissioner and providing mechanisms to seize traffickers' assets and use some of them towards compensating victims. Fiona Hill did a great deal of the work and she was a force to be reckoned with: *The Spectator* quoted a senior official describing a typical scene in Theresa's office: Fiona 'sitting back, getting ready to go out with her stockinged feet on the desk, giving a civil servant an absolute rollicking'.

Hill had to take a fairly brief break from Theresa's side due to the fallout from a ferocious row with the former Education Secretary – Nick Clegg once remarked that 'she rarely got on anything but badly with Michael Gove' and indeed the two had a history, of which more below. In 2014, Gove ordered the 'Trojan horse inquiry', an investigation into attempts to impose a hardline Sunni Islam agenda into some Birmingham schools. Led by former counterterrorism chief Peter Clarke, it found a 'sustained, coordinated agenda to impose segregationist attitudes and practices of a hardline, politicised strain of Sunni Islam [on children]. Left unchecked, it would confine schoolchildren within an intolerant, inward-looking monoculture that would severely inhibit their participation in the life of modern Britain.'

The fallout was immediate. 'Sources close to Gove' accused the Home Office and Charles Farr, who was by now in a relationship with Hill, of 'failing to drain the swamp of extremism' in Britain. The Home Office reacted by publishing confidential documents, which attacked Gove for failing to act on information about the Birmingham schools. Number 10 stepped in and forced Hill to resign for briefing against Gove; Gove himself was forced to apologise and was moved from Education. There were other reasons, but it created very bad blood and did nothing to endear Theresa and Gove to each other, least of all when both ran for the party leadership. Hill, meanwhile, went off to work in Lexington Communications, before being brought back into the fold.

But the tensions with Michael Gove went back much

further, for it was widely believed that after the 2010 election he felt that he, rather than Theresa, should have been given the Home Office brief. In 2006 he wrote a book called *Celsius 7/7*, published in the aftermath of the London bombings, in which he alleged that the West had allowed the extremist threat to get worse by appeasing fundamentalism, a charge levelled at, among others, the Home Office. He thus considered himself to be something of an expert on the subject and a few years later, during a meeting of the Extremism Task Force set up in the wake of the terrible murder of the British Army soldier, Fusilier Lee Rigby, tried to force Theresa, who was supported by Charles Farr, to take a more hardline approach.

She resisted and got her way, upon which Gove, still then on very close terms with David Cameron, went straight to the Prime Minister to press his own suit. Theresa inevitably found out, which did not do much to improve her opinion of him. Intriguingly, her view of him was as a schemer and conniver, not the public image at all until he stabbed Boris Johnson in the back in 2016, offering proof that she is a far shrewder judge of human nature than she is often given credit for.

The sometimes-bearded Nick Timothy is equally if not even more influential. Originally from Birmingham, he attended King Edward VI Aston Grammar School for Boys and it was his realisation that Labour would have shut the school down, had they won the 1992 General Election, that led him to join the Conservatives: 'I was twelve, and I had been at my grammar school for less than a year,' he recalled.

'I knew that if Labour won the election, my school would be closed down and the opportunity I had been given would be taken away. Thanks to the Tories, that did not happen and I became the first member of my family to go to university.'

The son of a steel worker and an alumnus of Sheffield University, where he studied politics, Timothy could not be less like the Bullingdon type if he tried. An avid Aston Villa supporter, at the time of writing he is engaged to Nike Trost, an official at the Financial Conduct Authority, and his influence on Theresa – who launched her leadership bid in Birmingham – cannot be underestimated.

Timothy started off in the insurance industry before moving to Conservative Research Department, where he was deputy director, overseeing a team of twenty policy advisers. He also worked for David Cameron in his Prime Minister's Questions team and moved to the Home Office when Theresa was appointed. A great admirer of Joseph Chamberlain, mayor of Birmingham in the 1870s – 'the Conservative Party's forgotten hero [who gave the party] an unambiguous mission: the betterment of Britain's working classes' – he wrote a book about his hero entitled *Our Joe: Joseph Chamberlain's Conservative Legacy*.

It was Timothy who was responsible for a famous speech Theresa gave to ConservativeHome in 2013, tellingly titled 'We Will Win By Being The Party For All', which very much foreshadowed the speech she made when ascending the steps of Number 10. The speech contained what was essentially a blueprint for a Theresa May-led government and provoked a great deal of attention, not least from David Cameron, because for the first time it became clear quite how high she was setting her sights. It kicked off with a commitment to get rid of the Human Rights Act because it curtailed the powers of government; it was: 'interfering with our ability to fight crime and control immigration. When Strasbourg constantly moves the goalposts and prevents the deportation of dangerous men like Abu Qatada, we have to ask ourselves, to what end are we signatories to the Convention? Are we really limiting human rights abuses in other countries? I'm sceptical. But are we restricting our ability to act in the national interest? So by 2015 we'll need a plan for dealing with the European Court of Human Rights. And yes, I want to be clear that all options – including leaving the Convention altogether – should be on the table'.

Theresa also had something to say about capitalism itself. Unlike many of her fellow politicians, she really appeared to understand the full extent of public anger about a banking system gone awry that had created a global recession and the huge and growing disparity between the captains of industry awarding themselves a small fortune in remuneration and everyone else. 'But believing in free markets doesn't mean we believe that anything goes, and it doesn't mean that capitalism, regardless of the form it takes, is always perfect,' she insisted. 'Where it's manifestly failing, where it's losing public support, where it's not helping to provide opportunity for all, we have to reform it. But the problems with the system go much wider and much deeper than the banking industry. There's Britain's over-reliance on financial services. Questions about our productivity and competitiveness. The crisis in our public finances. The inequality between London and the rest of the country. The cost of living. Stalling social mobility. The public's anger about companies that evade taxes and excessive corporate pay. All too often, the system doesn't seem to be working for the whole country.'

There was more – about the need to be globally competitive, about what the government could do to help industry, about building a small, strong, strategic state. Finally, Theresa vowed to 'reform capitalism [to] work for all of us'.

Well beyond her remit at the Home Office, the speech caused massive waves, with many seeing it as an attempt to snatch Labour's natural territory, although many more regarded it as a blatant bid to become the next Prime Minister. Twitter promptly labelled it as 'TM4PM'; it caused severe tensions with Number 10, although that was hotly denied amid assertions that David Cameron had approved it in advance.

But it may have been this speech that also forced Nick Timothy into a brief sabbatical period, although the blame was put in another episode. Along with Stephen Parkinson, he refused to campaign in the 2014 Rochester by-election on the grounds that as special advisers they were not allowed to; in return their names were taken off the Parliamentary Candidates list, leaving Timothy unable to stand for the Tories in the Aldridge-Brownhills constituency in Walsall. That was the ostensible reason, at any rate; many suspected that he in particular was being punished for encouraging Theresa to go too far. It is said neither of them ever really forgave Cameron for that and some of the sweeping changes Theresa made to the personnel on the front bench, especially the culling of the former Bullingdon members, can be traced directly to the animosity that began back then.

Nick Timothy left and in 2015 helped ensure the defeat of UKIP leader Nigel Farage to become MP for Thanet South. He then went on to work for the New Schools Network, a not-for-profit body promoting free schools. During his time in exile, he wrote a series of pieces for ConservativeHome, which reflected his own political philosophy. 'We need to keep asking ourselves what, in 2016, does the Conservative Party offer a working-class kid from Brixton, Birmingham, Bolton or Bradford? If we do that, we won't go far wrong,' was one such diatribe and again was uncannily close to what Theresa later said on the steps to Number 10. Some have, perhaps unkindly, called him 'Theresa May's brain' and it is certainly true that he and Fiona Hill were able to spot and head off serious potential troublesome scenarios, which helped keep her in the Home Office for so long. He wrote Theresa's speech for the 2015 Annual Conference and also came back to help her in running her leadership bid. 'Labour, in the pursuit of equality, only hold people back,' he once wrote, 'but it is the Conservatives who help you to go as far as your potential allows.'

Like Theresa, Timothy played a blinder during the 2016 referendum itself. He backed Brexit but was critical of the Leave campaign and, as such, that should reassure those who do not believe that Theresa will Brexit as comprehensively as the nation expects. Indeed the two are so close on policy matters that it's been commented, 'It's difficult to know where the overlap starts and stops.'

He is also full of praise for his boss. 'As long as I have known her she has always refused to allow herself to be pigeonholed by saying she is in this club or that club or on this wing or that wing of the party,' he told *The Spectator*. 'It confounds some people, it especially confounds the Left, that you can be so sceptical about the European Court of Human Rights, but you can care so passionately about the rights of the citizen. It confounds them that she thinks immigration needs to be much lower, at the same time as introducing the first legislation of its kind on modern slavery. I don't think that's inconsistent, I think that she's a sound Conservative who believes in social justice.'

Stephen Parkinson is the third of the trio. Originally from Tyneside (another non-Bullingdon), Parkinson read history at Emmanuel College, Cambridge, where he became president of the Union Society, which he also wrote a book about in 2009. He took up a post at the Conservative Research Department, and also worked for the Centre for Policy Studies and Conservative Central Office. A former lobbyist who worked for Quiller Consultants, he became part of the team briefing David

Cameron for Prime Minister's Questions and joined Theresa at the Home Office in 2012. Parkinson also had his name removed from the Approved Candidates list; he too will not have forgotten that in a hurry. He also went on to work on the Vote Leave campaign and again is a huge influence on Theresa.

***

In the background, of course, there was Philip. He rarely appeared in public during Theresa's tenure as Home Secretary, letting his wife get on with it as he continued to progress his own career. After working for de Zoete & Bevan, Prudential Portfolio Managers (where, as head of pension funds, he won an award at the Extels, known as the 'City's Oscars') and Deutsche Asset Management, which is where he ended up after Prudential bought rival M&G and then sold some of its fund management business to the German bank.

Philip moved to Capital International as a relationship manager around 2006. By the time Theresa became Prime Minister it was a giant, managing $1.4 trillion, including $20 billion worth of shares in Amazon and Starbucks, both singled out by Theresa when, as PM, she vowed to crack down on tax avoidance: 'We need to talk about tax. It doesn't matter to me whether you're Amazon, Google or Starbucks: you have a duty to put something back, you have a debt to your fellow citizens, you have a responsibility to pay your taxes. So as Prime Minister, I will crack down on individual and corporate tax avoidance and evasion.'

Capital International also owned large chunks in investment bank JP Morgan Chase & Co., defence outfit Lockheed Martin, Irish low-cost airline Ryanair, the pharmaceutical giant Merck & Co., Inc. and tobacco company Philip Morris, all of which could have been used to target Theresa by her political foes had her husband been responsible for picking any of them. But he wasn't.

It was important to emphasise that he was a relationship manager and not a fund manager: 'He is not involved with, and doesn't manage, money and is not a portfolio manager,' the firm made clear after Theresa became PM in July 2016. 'His job is to ensure the clients are happy with the service and that we understand their goals. Philip is not involved with our investment research or portfolio management activities.' In other words, he could not make investment decisions based on any snippet of government policy that he might have picked up on. After all Caesar's wife must be above suspicion.

Colleagues spoke well of him: 'He often chairs meetings and does a very good job of making sure that everybody has their say,' one told *The Guardian*. 'Around the office, he is a fairly head-down type of guy. There is a stereotypical investment manager with a big ego – he's not like that at all. He is fairly quiet, keeps himself to himself. He has very good integrity and never trades off his wife's name.'

There has never been a whiff of scandal about Theresa, but there has been one curious story that has never entirely gone away, although it is totally untrue. It is this: that Philip owns shares in G4S, the international security firm that has frequently been involved in governmental projects. The rumours first began on various blogs, but when they made it to Twitter, the company itself finally spoke out, tweeting, 'It's a bogus Twitter myth that Theresa May's husband owns shares in G4S.'

There was some bemusement that no one had sought to clarify that previously as the rumours had been around for some years and at one stage had been so widely believed that a petition was launched on Change.org. It attracted fewer than 9,000 signatures, all of them ill-informed because the petition was wrong, but it could have caused a major embarrassment. It read:

> Let us all remember that the woman responsible for cutting police budgets is Home Secretary Theresa May – whose husband is a major shareholder in G4S. Apparently the Parliamentary watchdogs don't think that's a serious conflict of interest but the rest of us should not be so blinkered. G4S are taking on more and more Police roles, as the Met Police budget shrinks Theresa May's husband picks up more business. How can this not be a conflict of interests? Theresa May should be removed.

Curiously, this was not Theresa's only brush with matters concerning G4S. Lincolnshire Police awarded the company a £200 million, ten-year contract in 2012. However, it then emerged that Tom Winsor, a partner at a law firm that worked for G4S, wrote an independent report about police reform for the British government in 2010.

At the Police Federation conference, a venue at which Theresa quite regularly had somewhat bruising encounters with the coppers, she was asked by delegate Sarah Adams, 'When you appointed Tom Winsor to carry out your independent review of policy, did you know that the law firm Tom Winsor is part of, which is White and Case, was negotiating the multi-million groundbreaking deal for G4S with Lincolnshire Police? How can it be fair and independent if there's a vested interest?'

'Tom Winsor did his review entirely independently. He did not do that review as part of the firm – he did it as an individual,' Theresa replied. 'You might not like all the answers that came out of the Winsor Review but there is a process whereby the Federation's voice will be heard in response to these proposals.'

A G4S spokesman was called in then as well, saying, 'There has been absolutely no conflict of interest: Mr Winsor has not been involved in any capacity with the legal team which advised us on our contract with Lincolnshire Police. Furthermore, no member of the G4S policing team has even had contact with Mr Winsor.'

Theresa was duly vindicated. She didn't add that she was a 'straight kinda gal' and that she was speaking honestly here, but then again she didn't need to: she was Theresa May.

14

HEAD GIRL AT THE HOME OFFICE

When Theresa May stepped down as Home Secretary to take up the post of Prime Minister in July 2016, she was the longest-serving incumbent in the post since James Chuter Ede over sixty years previously. Determined from the start to make her mark in the role, her three main policy areas comprised police reform, war on drugs and a harder line on immigration. In this last she did succeed in introducing some restrictions but Britain's membership of the EU, with its firm commitment to freedom of movement, made that last a very tricky area and one over which she might have far greater influence as PM. The Shadow Home Secretary before the election had in fact been Chris Grayling, but there was none of the animosity between the two of them that there was with Michael Gove (and several others) and when Theresa became PM she made him Secretary of State for Transport.

As recorded earlier in this book, the first thing Theresa did in the Home Office was to overturn Labour legislation concerning data collection and surveillance, getting rid of national identity cards and database schemes and restricting the retention of DNA samples while imposing controls on the use of CCTV cameras. Other early initiatives included scrapping the Labour 'go orders' initiative, which was supposed to protect women against domestic violence by banning abusers from the victim's home, as well as closing the ContactPoint database, which held information on all children under the age of eighteen in the UK. It was set up following the tragic death of the eight-year-old Victoria Climbié in 2000, but was of serious concern to many on the grounds of invasion of privacy, breaching doctor-patient confidentiality and the growth of surveillance society, yet another of the toxic Labour legacies that the Conservatives had to overturn on attaining office.

Other early initiatives included the speech to the Association of Police Officers, mentioned elsewhere, a review of counter-terrorism legislation and banning a march by the English Defence League (EDL). There was also that flirtation with the idea of using water cannon during rioting, which Theresa subsequently decided against when rioting began again the following summer. In August 2011 there was widespread disturbance following the fatal shooting by police of a Tottenham resident called Mark Duggan, who had a very troubled past and who the police thought was going to shoot at them. As he was black, a racial element was involved. A protest march took place a couple of days later, but it turned into rioting and looting in Tottenham, violence which sparked further disturbances in Brixton, Enfield, Islington, Wood Green and Oxford Circus, in the very centre of the capital.

Subsequently rioting spread further across London with at least two deaths and then across to further areas in Britain, including Birmingham, where shots were fired at a police helicopter and petrol bombs thrown at officers. There were more fatalities as violence spread to Leicester, the West Midlands, Liverpool and Manchester, with the perpetrators helping to organise the disruption by use of social media and increasingly inflamed accounts of Mark Duggan's death. By the time it quietened down there had been deaths and injuries, including a seventy-five-year-old woman suffering a broken hip and a Malaysian student who was beaten and robbed by a group of thugs who had been pretending to help him. There was also terrible damage to property, with at least a hundred homes destroyed, buses set on fire, commercial properties destroyed and the cancellation of various sporting fixtures.

Theresa had been on holiday when the riots broke out: she returned immediately amid claims that extremist organisations such as the English Defence League (EDL) and the British National Party (BNP) were trying to capitalise on the riots in a bid to increase support. By then she had changed her mind about the use of water cannon: 'The way we police in Britain is not through use of water cannon. The way we police in Britain is through consent of communities. I condemn utterly the violence in Tottenham. Such disregard for public safety and property will not be tolerated, and the Metropolitan Police have my full support in restoring order.'

The rioters were not merely violent, they weren't the brightest in the bunch either, which meant that many were clearly identifiable as they had not bothered to cover their faces. Theresa was all for naming and shaming, no matter how young: 'When I was in Manchester last week, the issue was raised to me about the anonymity of juveniles who are found guilty of crimes of this sort,' she said. 'The Crown Prosecution Service is to order prosecutors to apply for anonymity to be lifted in any youth case they think is in the public interest. The law currently protects the identity of any suspect under the age of eighteen, even if they are convicted, but it also allows for an application to have such restrictions lifted, if deemed appropriate.' She added that 'What I've asked for is that CPS guidance should go to prosecutors to say that where possible, they should be asking for the anonymity of juveniles who are found guilty of criminal activity to be lifted.'

This was not the last time the question of using water cannon came up. In 2014, as Mayor of London, Boris Johnson sanctioned the purchase of three second-hand German water cannon, only to be comprehensively slapped down by Theresa on the grounds that they were faulty and needed repair and in any case were too dangerous to use whatever their condition. Citing the case of a sixty-six-year-old Stuttgart resident who was blinded by a water cannon, she said, 'Where the medical and scientific evidence suggests those powers could cause serious harm, where the operational case is not clear, and where the historic principle of policing by consent could be placed at risk, I will not give my agreement. The application for the authorisation of the Wasserwerfer 9000 water cannon does not meet that high threshold.'

That added Johnson to the list of big beasts she was unafraid to take on (and also gave him a taste of what she could be like to deal with), but the toxicity that existed between herself and Gove was not present here. Boris, much to the surprise of many, was to get one of the biggest jobs under the new May regime. It also won her the approval of some of the UK's largest police forces, who did not wish to deploy the cannon, as well as that of the human rights organisation Liberty.

Theresa ruled out a public inquiry into the phone-tapping scandal but made a rare well-shod misstep at the Conservative Party Conference of 4 October 2011, when talking about the need to reform the Human Rights Act, saying the meaning of Article 8 had been 'perverted'. She cited a foreign national who was allowed to remain in the UK, 'We all know the stories about the Human Rights Act, about the illegal immigrant who cannot be deported because – and I am not making this up – he had a pet cat.' The Royal Courts of Justice (RCJ) denied this, saying that he was in a genuine relationship with a British partner, and the pet was proof the relationship was 'genuine' and 'had nothing to do with' the judgement.

Amnesty International said her comments only fuelled 'myths and misconceptions' about the Human Rights Act: 'That someone in Theresa May's position can be so misinformed as to parade out a story about someone being allowed to stay in Britain because of a cat is nothing short of alarming.'

Ken Clarke, at that point Justice Secretary, called the speech 'laughable and childlike' in the latest of their run-ins. 'I sat and listened to Theresa's speech and I'll have to be very polite to Theresa when I meet her, but in my opinion she should really address her researchers and advisers very severely for assuring her that a complete nonsense example in her speech was true,' he told the *Nottingham Post*. 'I'm not going to stand there and say in my private opinion this is a terrible thing and we ought to get rid of the Human Rights Act.' William Hague, the Foreign Secretary, was forced to intervene, claiming the two were 'on the same page'.

There was more trouble from the EDL in the wake of the murder of Drummer Lee Rigby. They organised a march in Woolwich, south-east London, where the soldier had been killed in broad daylight in May 2013, and invited Pamela Geller and Robert Spencer, two American bloggers who co-founded the anti-Muslim group Stop Islamization of America, to speak. This potential cause for violent confrontation led the pressure group Hope not Hate to warn about them entering the country: Theresa duly banned Geller and Spencer from entering the UK. They were 'inflammatory speakers who promote hate,' according to the Home Office.

One of her biggest areas, touched on earlier in this book, was the speech she made on 26 July 2010, outlining her plans for police reform, including some heavy cost-cutting. In the wake of the economic chaos caused by Labour and the appalling state of the nation's finances, austerity was now the order of the day and the Home Office was included in this. There were also to be organisational reforms. The Serious Organised Crime Agency (SOCA), Labour's central crime agency, was to be replaced by a new National Crime Agency. There would be a bigger role for civilian 'reservists' for crime control.

The Home Office reforms were to produce a very positive result. By July 2013, crime had fallen by more than 10 per cent, occasioning, unsurprisingly, some glee. Theresa didn't do glee, however, and so instead her statement was delivered in a tone of cool satisfaction: 'These statistics show that our police reforms are continuing to deliver results across the country, with falls in crime in every police force in England and Wales,' she announced. 'Recorded crime is down by more than ten per cent under this government, and the independent survey shows that the public's experience of crime is at its lowest level since records began. This is a significant achievement. Police forces have shown an impressive ability to rise to the challenge of making savings while still cutting crime. This government has played its part by slashing red tape and scrapping targets to enable the police to focus on crime fighting. We have encouraged chief constables to make savings in back offices to give renewed focus on the frontline and we are seeing the benefits of those efficiencies. We have also set up a College of Policing to ensure the police are better equipped with the knowledge and skills they need to fight crime. England and Wales are safer than they have been for decades, but we will continue to improve our national crime fighting capability when the National Crime Agency is fully operational later this year.'

In June 2012, there was another rare setback when Theresa was found in contempt of court by Judge Barry Cotter, accused of 'totally unacceptable and regrettable behaviour' in the case of a legal agreement to free an Algerian from a UK Immigration Detention Centre. She eventually caved in; not to have done so would have incurred fines or imprisonment.

In July 2013, she decided to ban the stimulant khat, which was used in Somali, Yemeni and Ethiopian communities, sold in small shops and cafés in little bundles costing between £3 and £6. It was to be treated as a class C drug along the lines of anabolic steroids and ketamine, against the advice of the Advisory Council on the Misuse of Drugs (ACMD), which said there was 'insufficient evidence' it caused health problems. Theresa did not agree: 'The decision to bring khat under control is finely balanced and takes into account the expert scientific advice and these broader concerns,' she said, adding that it had already been banned in the majority of other EU member states, as well as most of the G8 countries including Canada and the US. 'Failure to take decisive action and change the UK's legislative position on khat would place the UK at a serious risk of becoming a single, regional hub for the illegal onward trafficking,' she continued.

As always there was opposition elsewhere. Niamh Eastwood, executive director at drug policy campaigners Release, said: 'Once again the Government chooses to ignore the evidence when it comes to drug policy. The ACMD recommended that khat should not be banned, and this has been ignored. There is no evidence that criminalisation has any tangible effect on the rates of drug use in a society.' But Theresa had her way.

That was also the month of one of her greatest triumphs. On 7 July 2013, Abu Qatada, a radical cleric arrested in 2002, who had been fighting deportation ever since, was deported to Jordan after a decade-long battle that had cost the nation £1.7 million in legal fees. Ever since 2002, a succession of home secretaries had been battling to get him out and Theresa was finally able to do so as the result of a treaty she negotiated in April 2013, under which Jordan agreed to give Qatada a fair trial and to refrain from torturing him.

She is justly proud of this, crowing in September 2013 that 'he will not be returning to the UK', and pointing out in her 2016 leadership campaign announcement that she was told that she 'couldn't deport Abu Qatada' but that she 'flew to Jordan and negotiated the treaty that got him out of Britain for good'. This played a big role in shaping her views on the European Convention on Human Rights and European Court of Human Rights. They had 'moved the goalposts' and had a 'crazy interpretation of our human rights laws'.

Theresa was similarly tough elsewhere. In November 2013 the Supreme Court overturned Jacqui Smith's revocation of Iraqi-born terror suspect Al Jedda's British citizenship. Theresa's response was to order it to be revoked for a second time, making him the first person to be twice stripped of British citizenship.

The inner steel glinted again when Theresa was accused by Lord Roberts of being willing to allow someone to die 'to score a political point' over the deportation of a mentally ill Nigerian man called Isa Muazu. According to his lawyer, Theresa had arranged for Muazu, said to be 'near death' after a hundred-day hunger strike, to be deported by a chartered private jet. An 'end of life' plan was reportedly offered to Muazu, who was one of a number of hunger strikers at the Harmondsworth Immigration Removal Centre, a clear indication that the Home Office was in no mood to be conciliatory to those they could actually deport.

In 2014, there was another sermon in the guise of a speech to the Police Federation, which was getting used to regular tickings-off from the Head Girl in the Home Office. This time police culture came under attack: 'When you remember the list of recent revelations about police misconduct, it is not enough to mouth platitudes about "a few bad apples", she said with a note of scorn. 'The problem might lie with a minority of officers, but it is still a significant problem, and a problem that needs to be addressed. According to one survey carried out recently, only 42 per cent of black people from a Caribbean background trust the police. That is simply not sustainable. I will soon publish proposals to strengthen the protections available to whistleblowers in the police. I am creating a new criminal offence of police corruption. And I am determined that the use of stop and search must come down, become more targeted and lead to more arrests.'

This is one of the best-known of Theresa's speeches, requiring as it did some nerve to take on the established forces of policing, and it greatly enhanced her standing among both colleagues and the public. It was one of the successes she was able to cite when campaigning to become PM.

In March 2014, Theresa incurred some raised eyebrows when she signed a secret security pact with Saudi Arabia's Crown Prince Mohammed bin Nayef, and in 2015 she supported a £5.9 million contract to help run prisons in Saudi Arabia, which was opposed by Justice Secretary Michael Gove and by Labour Party leader Jeremy Corbyn.

Later that year she saw off someone else who clearly considered her to be a 'bloody difficult woman'. In November Liberal Democrat Norman Baker, serving in the Home Office as the crime prevention minister, resigned, laying the blame entirely at Theresa's door. In the wake of a bitter clash over a delay in publishing a Home Office report on drugs policies abroad, he told *The Independent* that working at the Home Office was like, 'walking through mud. They have looked upon it as a Conservative department in a Conservative government, whereas in my view it's a Coalition department in a Coalition government. That mindset has framed things, which means I have had to work very much harder to get things done even where they are what the Home Secretary agrees with and where it has been helpful for the Government and the department. There comes a point when you don't want to carry on walking through mud and you want to release yourself from that.'

In his resignation letter to Nick Clegg he commented that, 'I regret that in the Home Office, the goodwill to work collegiately to take forward rational evidence-based policy has been in somewhat short supply.'

In 2015, to the surprise of many, the Conservatives won the General Election with an outright majority, gaining 24 seats to claim 330 in total. The election changed the political landscape: the Liberal Democrats were all but wiped out, falling to the status of fourth party, losing 49 seats and ending up with just 8. Labour, under the hapless Ed Miliband, lost 26 seats and ended up with 232, while in Scotland, the SNP under another tough woman, Nicola Sturgeon, swept the board, shooting up from 6 seats to 56 out of a total of 59, ending up as the third largest party.

This essentially destroyed a chance of Labour forming a government in the near future because with the exception of the Blair years, Labour has always needed Scotland in order to secure a majority. It then started the process of self-destruction that involved getting rid of Miliband and installing someone even worse, Jeremy Corbyn, in his stead. Back in Scotland, meanwhile, yet another tough woman emerged, one Ruth Davidson, the head of the Scottish Conservative Party, which for the first time in decades looked to be the real party of opposition to the SNP.

David Cameron at last became Prime Minister sans Clegg and some of the senior personnel remained in situ: Osborne was still Chancellor and Theresa stayed on at the Home Office – by that time it was very apparent quite what a success she'd made of the role – while Philip Hammond remained as Foreign Secretary, having taken over from William Hague in 2014. Freed from the constricts of having to act in agreement with the Lib Dems, he returned to legislation involving increased surveillance powers, immediately and inevitably dubbed the 'snooper's charter'. This aimed to make internet and mobile service providers keep records of internet usage, voice calls, messages and email for up to a year in case police requested access to the records while investigating a crime.

Theresa lost no time in telling the BBC why she had previously been unable to act: 'David Cameron has already said, and I've said, that a Conservative government would be giving the security agencies and law-enforcement agencies the powers that they need to ensure they're keeping up to date as people communicate with communications data,' she said. 'We were prevented from bringing in that legislation into the last government because of the coalition with the Liberal Democrats and we are determined to bring that through, because we believe that is necessary to maintain the capabilities for our law-enforcement agencies such that they can continue to do the excellent job, day in and day out, of keeping us safe and secure.'

This drew a very frosty response from the human rights watchdog, Privacy International. 'Raising the spectre of expanded surveillance powers only moments after the election results have emerged is a clear indication of the forthcoming assault on the rights of ordinary British citizens,' said Carly Nyst, PI's legal director. 'Theresa May's comments confirm that widespread public concern about the threats posed to online privacy and expression by internet monitoring powers has been completely ignored by the new government. Communications data legislation has been repeatedly criticised by experts and politicians from all reaches of the political spectrum, and has been beaten back by the public and civil society time and time again. Reviving it as a policy priority is a clear sign both of an insatiable appetite for spying powers, and intentions to continue to sacrifice the civil liberties of Britons everywhere on the altar of national security.' This was not the view of the wider public, however. The heightened threat of Islamic extremist-led terrorism, both at home and abroad, was leading many to feel that the government had to act.

The one area in which it was almost impossible to implement

the wishes of the people was, of course, immigration, beyond a doubt the reason why the majority of the country voted to leave the EU. In 2010 Theresa had promised to bring the level of net migration down to less than 100,000, but this was to prove impossible and in February 2015, *The Independent* reported, 'The Office for National Statistics (ONS) announced a net flow of 298,000 migrants to the UK in the 12 months to September 2014 – up from 210,000 in the previous year.' However, she did act where she could. She rejected the EU's proposal of compulsory refugee quotas, caused by the ongoing crisis of migrants coming from the Middle East and North Africa: 'When a new piece of legislation in the area of justice and home affairs – including asylum policy – is proposed, the UK can choose whether or not to participate in it. We will not participate in any legislation imposing a mandatory system of resettlement or relocation,' the Home Office announced. Theresa added that it was important to help people living in war-zone regions and refugee camps but 'not the ones who are strong and rich enough to come to Europe'.

On 11 June 2012, she announced that new restrictions would be introduced, intended to reduce the number of non-European Economic Area family migrants. From 9 July 2012 only British citizens earning more than £18,600 could bring their spouse or their child to live with them in the UK, a figure that would rise significantly in cases where visa applications are also made for children, while the two-year probationary period for partners was increased to five years. The rules also prevented any adult and elderly dependents from settling in the UK unless they can demonstrate that, as a result of age, illness or disability, they require a level of long-term personal care that can only be provided by a relative in the UK.

It was a beginning, but it was not enough and it is only after Brexit has started for good that Theresa's government will finally be able to stop the influx of immigrants into the country, a long-held desire of many British people that has been shamefully ignored for decades. History will judge.

During her time in office, and very much against her natural instincts, Theresa has had to go public on two highly personal topics, recognising that in today's social media-led world, politicians must open up on subjects that they could previously have ignored. The first is the issue of childlessness, which should never have been brought up as an issue at any time, let alone during the campaign for the party leadership, given that it is a deeply personal subject that no one should be forced to explain. But in this day and age, you do.

And so in an interview with the *Daily Telegraph* in 2012, she tackled it for the first time. 'It just didn't happen,' she explained. 'This isn't something I generally go into, but things just turned out as they did. You look at families all the time and you see there is something there that you don't have.' And there the matter should have rested, but it did not.

Theresa has also had to admit publicly to suffering from Type 1 diabetes, which was also diagnosed in 2012, having previously been diagnosed as having Type 2. This meant her medication had to be changed from tablets to two self-administered insulin injections a day, something she tackled with her usual brisk pragmatism. 'My very first reaction was that it's impossible because at my age you don't get it,' she told the charity Diabetes UK. 'But, then my reaction was: "Oh no, I'm going to have to inject" and thinking about what that would mean in practical terms. I hadn't appreciated the degree of management it requires and I hadn't appreciated, for example, the paradox that while everyone assumes diabetes is about not eating sugar, if you have a hypo, then you have to take something that's got that high glucose content.'

In fact, Theresa became pretty much the poster girl by showing how anyone could lead a high-powered life while suffering from diabetes: 'I go to a lot of functions where I am eating and I speak at dinners, so that brings an added complication,' she continued. 'When I'm going to do a debate or speaking at a conference, I have to make sure that I've tested and know where I am, so I can adjust as necessary. There was one occasion when I had been expecting to go into the Chamber later, but the way the debates were drawn up meant I had to go in at eleven a.m. and I knew I wasn't coming out till about five. I had a bag of nuts in my handbag and one of my colleagues would lean forward every now and then, so that I could eat some nuts without being seen by the Speaker.'

Theresa is aware of her ice maiden reputation and there have been some attempts to thaw out, as when in November 2014 she went on BBC Radio 4's *Desert Island Discs* and chose as her luxury a subscription to *Vogue* magazine. She has also revealed a collection of a hundred cookery books and says she likes to experiment with her cooking. But it is her professional life that has dominated all.

Theresa's record as Home Secretary has been an exemplary one and provides clear evidence that she has been prime ministerial material from the start. From tackling vested interests to taking on some of her fellow big beasts in government, she has been far bolder than her reputation as a cautious woman – 'Theresa May – and then again she may not' – would lead people to believe. But it is the biggest challenge of them all that awaited Prime Minister May – that of taking Britain out of the EU.

15

HEADMISTRESS
AT NUMBER 10

As the sense of shock over the result of the EU referendum began to subside, it was replaced by an almost palpable feeling of relief over the identity of the new Prime Minister. As Labour continued on its path of self-destruction, the Conservatives had done what they were best at: pulled themselves together fast and turned themselves back into an efficient election-winning machine. They had chosen by far the best candidate as PM and the country knew it too: there was a palpable sense that after the teenage boys had been running rampant, a grown-up had taken over. And this did seem to be the age of the strong woman: with Nicola Sturgeon and Ruth Davidson battling it out in Scotland, Angela Merkel running Europe from Germany, and Hillary

Clinton standing as the Democratic candidate for the US presidency, Theresa May was in good company.

On 13 July 2016, Theresa became the UK's second female Prime Minister and the very nature of the government changed overnight. First, there was a bloodbath of the Bullingdons: David Cameron was leaving voluntarily, of course, but Chancellor George Osborne was out, having spent the previous weeks hinting that he might be prepared to accept another senior position, should it come his way. It didn't. Michael Gove, who appeared to have scuttled off with his tail between his legs since his knifing of Boris Johnson, was nowhere to be seen. Privilege gave way to pragmatism as the new PM put her Cabinet in place.

The scale of the change stunned some people: the safe and dependable Philip Hammond became Chancellor, Amber Rudd, MP for Hastings and Rye since 2010, was given the unenviable job of following Theresa at the Home Office and in a move that stunned some onlookers, Boris Johnson became Foreign Secretary. It was a little unfortunate that in the course of the referendum campaign he had compared the EU's aims to those of Hitler and Napoleon and that he'd been openly accused by his French counterpart, Jean-Marc Ayrault, of lying, but no matter. It was, in actual fact, a very smart move. Theresa had put him in a position in which, if he performed well, he would owe it to her and would be in no position to be disloyal, and if he failed, he would do so in the full glare of the global limelight and end up a busted flush.

Former Shadow Home Secretary David Davis was brought back into the government as Cabinet Secretary for exiting the EU and Liam Fox made head of a new international trade department, a crucial role in the run-up to leaving. Both men were ardent Brexiters, allaying fears in some corners that Britain wouldn't Brexit after all. Andrea Leadsom got the farming ministry and with it the problem of working out how the UK farmers would replace lost EU agricultural subsidies.

One immediate concern was when to trigger Article 50, the means by which a member state leaves the EU. Exiting PM David Cameron refused to do it and Theresa made it clear that she wouldn't be pushed into it either, stressing the need for a 'UK approach', which meant somehow getting Scotland on board. Some onlookers were perplexed when one of Theresa's first acts as Prime Minister was to travel to Scotland to meet SNP leader Nicola Sturgeon, but the Scots had voted to stay in the EU 62 to 38 per cent and pragmatism was again called for to keep the Union – the Union between England, Scotland, Wales and Northern Ireland, that is – intact. There was some early grandstanding from Sturgeon about being able to put a stop to Brexit but Theresa soon squashed that.

But now that she was the head of government Theresa could turn her mind to other matters and one of the first things she did as PM was to signal that the eighteen-year ban on grammar schools might come to an end. The thinking of her 'brain' Nick Timothy, he who became a Tory when it became clear to him that Labour would have been a threat to his own grammar school, was clearly evident, but Theresa herself was a grammar-school girl – and look where it had got her. The matter of selective education, or grammar schools, was a very divisive one and anathema to Labour – not that anyone other than a tiny minority were listening to them any more – but no one could deny that the schools system in Britain was not fit for purpose.

Once the envy of half the world, education in Britain had become a source of national shame, but David Cameron, with his hyper-privileged background, would not have risked bringing back the grammar schools himself, because he would have been accused of elitism. An ordinary middle-class woman whose grandparents had been in domestic service was in an entirely different position, however. One of the arguments against grammar schools had been that at the too-young age of eleven pupils had been forced to sit the 11-plus, an exam that would have a direct bearing on the rest of their lives, with those who passed going on to a grammar and those who failed condemned to a secondary modern.

One early suggestion was that the all-important exam should be taken when the child was a year or two older, a suggestion backed by Conservative Voice, an influential group set up in 2012 by David Davis and Liam Fox. 'Not everything about the previous system of grammar schools was desirable,' Conservative Voice co-founder Don Porter told the *Daily Telegraph*. 'For example, we believe that the testing of a child only at the age of eleven was far too restrictive. In future, we recommend continual testing to enable children who develop at a later stage to benefit from a grammar school education. It [the 11-plus] is a one-off. Not everybody is ready to determine whether they are right for grammar school level at eleven. Why can't we open it up at 12, 13, 14, 15 and have this continual opportunity for people to have another go at getting in?'

In a letter to Theresa and Education Secretary Justine Greening he added, 'The first wave of new grammar schools should be placed in areas of the country facing social deprivation', and there should also be a 'higher standard of technical education for those students who do not wish to pursue an academic path'.

Another example of Theresa's supremely pragmatic nature, allied with a willingness to take on controversial subjects, is her take on fracking, the process by which gas and oil is extracted from shale rock. According to a British Geological Survey (BGS) estimate, there may be around 40 trillion cubic metres of shale gas in northern England alone, with just 10 per cent of the UK's shale reserves able to provide the nation's energy for fifty years. Enthusiasts have said it has transformed the US economy, where fracking has been going on for over a decade, creating an estimated million jobs and slashing both energy bills and greenhouse gas emissions. It has long been considered the future of the energy industry in some quarters and equally violently opposed in others, concerned about its environmental impact. Fracking remains a polarising issue.

Theresa has sought a supremely practical way of dealing with the people most affected: money. This was not an entirely new idea; in 2015 a shale wealth fund was created to set aside up to 10 per cent of tax proceeds from fracking to benefit the communities that will have the wells in their midst.

Initially it was assumed that these funds would go to communities and local trusts (George Osborne's idea) but the new Prime Minister had a far more effective solution – pay the money directly to the individual and it is predicted each affected community could receive up to £10 million, with individual households looking at about £10,000, although the final figures are not clear at the time of writing. Somewhat predictably environmental campaigners promptly referred to these payments as 'bribes'.

But Theresa did not agree. 'The government I lead will be always be driven by the interests of the many – ordinary families for whom life is harder than many people in politics realise,' she said, speaking ahead of the consultation launch. 'As I said on my first night as Prime Minister, when we take the big calls, we'll think not of the powerful but of you. This announcement is an example of putting those principles into action. It's about making sure people personally benefit from economic decisions that are taken – not just councils – and putting them back in control over their lives. We'll be looking at applying this approach to other government programmes in the future too, as we press on with the work of building a country that works for everyone.'

It was a theme she was to return to repeatedly.

Nick Timothy's influence showed through in another hugely controversial area, that of Chinese involvement in nuclear power. Anyone who knew of either Timothy's views or indeed Theresa's acceptance of them should have looked at a piece he wrote for the ConservativeHome website in November 2015 when the Chinese President Xi was visiting Britain: 'During Xi's visit to London, the two governments will sign deals giving Chinese state-owned companies stakes in the British nuclear power stations planned for Hinkley Point in Somerset and Sizewell in Suffolk. It is believed that the deals could lead to the Chinese designing and constructing a third nuclear reactor at Bradwell in Essex. Security experts – reportedly inside as well as outside government – are worried that the Chinese could use their role to build weaknesses into computer systems which will allow them to shut down Britain's energy production at will.'

It should therefore have been of no surprise to anyone that towards the end of July, very much at the eleventh hour, the new Prime Minister ordered a review of the £18 billion project involving the nuclear power station at Hinkley Point, another key Osborne policy that Theresa seemed only too happy to bin. There were mutterings from within the government that Osborne had failed to 'read the small print'. Nick Timothy, more bearded than ever, commented that it was 'baffling that "hostile" China had been invited to invest in key infrastructure projects'.

There was an immediate backlash from the unions ('bewildering and bonkers,' said GMB union boss Justin Bowden) and also from the British Chambers of Commerce. China itself, meanwhile, was livid, with the Chinese ambassador to Britain, Liu Xiaoming, quoted in the *Financial Times*: 'The China-UK relationship is at a crucial historical juncture. Mutual trust should be treasured even more. I hope the UK will keep its door open to China and that the British government will continue to support Hinkley Point – and come to a decision as soon as possible so that the project can proceed smoothly.' The language was diplomatic but some took this to mean that if the UK didn't play ball, it might also affect the Chinese approach to Brexit.

Lord (Peter) Mandelson, who just happens to be president of the Great Britain China Centre, which promotes closer Anglo-Chinese relations, also popped up to sniff that Brexit meant Britain 'can't be too fussy about who we do trade with' and added that it would be 'globally suicidal' for China to interfere in another country's defences. 'Nobody would trust Chinese investment again, nobody would want to do business with China again,' he told BBC Radio 4's *Today* programme. 'In the round the government has to consider China's motivation for wanting to get into financing projects like this. In my view, and I guess in their view too, they judge that it would be commercially, globally suicidal for China if they were to invest on the one hand and then try to mess around with other countries' security the next. The truth is that China would have far, far too much to lose if it were to start compromising other countries' national security.'

At the time of writing it is still not clear what the outcome of the review will be.

***

Theresa and Philip are partial to Alpine walks, and headed to Switzerland (Margaret Thatcher's favoured destination) for a break in the summer of 2016 before beginning business proper at the annual Tory Party conference, her first as Prime Minister, and then the nitty-gritty of negotiating Brexit. The two are fond of Lucerne, the Bernese Oberland and Zermatt, which affords views of the Matterhorn.

'My husband and I discovered the joys of walking in Switzerland quite by chance,' she told the *Daily Telegraph* in 2007. 'We first visited the country about twenty-five years ago. On a return trip, we decided to go walking, enjoyed it and gradually began doing more adventurous hikes. The views are spectacular, the air is clear and you can get some peace and quiet; the key thing is to go well prepared – and invest in a good pair of walking boots.'

It was an early sign that there would be no Cameron-style display of holidaying in Britain (although the new PM does favour the Welsh hills) –but some wags did point out that Switzerland is not a part of the EU.

It is accurately said that the first hundred days defines a person's leadership and on that showing Theresa May has so far been a success. Exuding natural authority, she has emphasised the need for 'blue collar' Conservatism, the need to address the issues of working men and women as well as a class that many somewhat unfairly consider themselves born to rule. But there are pitfalls ahead and many of them relate to her own party.

Theresa was not afraid to conduct her own night of the long knives, but in doing so she has ruffled a few feathers, not least those of George Osborne, a chancellor whose remit stretched far beyond his own department, by rejecting or amending some of his key policy areas. Just before her first Cabinet meeting, the new PM announced she was going to focus on 'improving productivity' and creating 'a plan to drive growth up and down the country – from rural areas to our great cities'. It was a direct slap in the face to Osborne, who has been criticised for failing to promote productivity and also for focusing on the so-called 'Northern powerhouse'.

Not for the first (or last) time, the PM focused on her election speech: 'As I said on my first day as Prime Minister, I will govern for the whole United Kingdom, and we will look to build an economy that works for everyone, not just the privileged few,' she announced. 'That is why we need a proper industrial strategy that focuses on improving productivity, rewarding hard-working people with higher wages and creating more opportunities for young people so that, whatever their background, they go as far as their talents will take them. We also need a plan to drive growth up and down the country – from rural areas to our great cities. If we are to take advantage of the opportunities presented by Brexit, we need to have our whole economy firing. That's why this Committee's work is of the highest priority, and we will be getting down to work immediately.'

It is unlikely that George Osborne or any of his peers in the old guard will make trouble in the shorter term, not least as it could damage their own standing in the party. Indeed, Osborne, who arguably suffered more than anyone from the referendum result as he had, by his own admission, put everything on the line, was not offered a Cabinet job under the new regime and has watched as his policies have been dismantled, has been surprisingly chipper. Delivering the annual Margaret Thatcher Lecture to the Centre for Policy Studies at London's Guildhall in July he said, 'As you all know, I fought hard – as hard as I could – for a different outcome to the referendum we have just held on our membership of the EU. I didn't do it by half measures, I couldn't on an issue like that. I put everything on the line, and don't regret for a moment that I did. But while I don't resile from any of the concerns that I expressed in advance of that vote, nor do I intend to re-run the arguments now the vote has passed. Tonight, and in the future, Theresa May and the new team she has assembled will have my support. She has the strength and the integrity to do the job, as she faces up to the great challenge that lies ahead.'

He called upon Theresa to stick with David Cameron's

commitments to spend 2 per cent of national income on defence and 0.7 per cent on international aid, the latter echoed by the former Prime Minister himself, who publicly asked his successor not to change this policy. But international aid is one of the great areas of controversy in both the party and the nation: ring-fenced from austerity measures and awarded to countries such as India, which have not only a booming economy but a space programme as well, it may well turn out to be a commitment too far.

The new PM also refused to involve herself in the row surrounding David Cameron's controversial Resignation Honours list and at the time of writing has resisted calls for a snap election, correctly judging that in the wake of the referendum the country needs a break from going to the polls. There is another good reason to wait, too. In 2018, boundary changes are expected to be finalised – something else David Cameron was unable to do after Nick Clegg reneged on his commitment – and even without taking the Labour meltdown into account could deliver an extra 48 seats to the Tories. Add in the Labour chaos and it is predicted that the new Prime Minister could end up with a 90-seat majority, rather than the 12-seat majority that Cameron returned. Early opinion ratings also put Theresa massively ahead of Labour leader Jeremy Corbyn in the polls. But if a week is a long time in politics, two years can cause huge upheavals.

Will Theresa May be as spectacularly successful as Britain's first female Prime Minister? Only history can say.